UNDERSTANDING
the HISTORICAL
LANDSCAPE

in its

ENVIRONMENTAL
SETTING

EDITED BY

T.C. SMOUT

 the **centre** for
environmental history
and **policy**

 Royal
Commission on the
Ancient and
Historical
Monuments of
Scotland

SCOTTISH CULTURAL PRESS

Contents

List of Contributors

JEAN BALFOUR, Farmer, landowner and former Chairman of the Countryside Commission for Scotland

L. DYSON BRUCE, formerly Royal Commission on the Ancient and Historical Monuments of Scotland

CAROLINE EARWOOD, Forest Enterprise in Wales

ALAN HAMPSON, Scottish Natural Heritage

R. HINGLEY, Department of Archaeology, University of Durham

H.A.P. INGRAM, Department of Geography, University of Dundee

LESLEY MACINNES, Historic Scotland

ROGER MERCER, Secretary of the Royal Commission on the Ancient and Historical Monuments of Scotland

CHRIS SMOUT, Centre for Environmental History and Policy, University of St Andrews

J.B. STEVENSON, Royal Commission on the Ancient and Historical Monuments of Scotland

Introduction

Much work is being undertaken in Scotland and elsewhere in the British Isles on landscape. The impetus comes from many directions. Academic geographers are deepening our understanding of the many subjective meanings that different people at various times read into their physical surroundings. Countryside planners are concerned about balancing the erosion of what is considered beautiful and interesting (and tourist-attracting) against job-creating development: where do you draw the line in landscape preservation? Archaeologists are less concerned with the grand sweep of land forms, or even the pylons on the skyline, than with the subtle, and often to the untutored eye virtually invisible, cultural landscapes with traces of former ages.

At the same time, various public agencies pursue their different responsibilities towards the landscape. Scottish Natural Heritage has undertaken a massive Landscape Character Assessment of the Scottish regions, dedicated especially to teasing out and describing the nature of the physical landscape resource: not least, this is a tool for the planners to enable prioritisation in difficult situations. The Forestry Commission wrestles both with the problems of forest design to make their plantations (and those of others) less of an affront, and also with the problems of conserving the archaeological heritage embedded in their woods. Historic Scotland and the Royal Commission on the Ancient and Historical Monuments of Scotland (RCAHMS) are charged with the duty of conserving and recording (respectively) the archaeological heritage wherever it may be found in their country.

The seven chapters in this book originated in a conference held at the SNH Countryside Centre at Battleby, Perthshire, which focussed especially on the problems of the cultural landscape as it exists in its environmental setting. Behind it was an agenda to improve dialogue – to show what needs to be done to persuade authority to consider the less visible landscape more seriously; to highlight specific problems from different perspectives; to demonstrate some of the efforts the agencies are making to understand the cultural landscape; and to illustrate the ways in which scientists and historical scholars can enrich each other's understanding and management of the landscape.

Roger Mercer's chapter provides an introductory overview 'of how the European west has seen landscape through history, sometimes with apprehension, often with delight, but never the same everywhere and at all times. We see it through eyes conditioned by our own time, and the dominant image of the countryside historically has generally been that formed by an urban elite visiting the country, but not having to live off it. The more we know at any time, the deeper we may choose to see. The work of the archaeologist, he suggests, always discovers aspects of landscape hitherto unappreciated. Not least, it is now capable of transforming how we see the Highlands: the common view formed by the romanticism of Scott and Landseer is still of 'Europe's last wilderness', but the uplands bear witness to thousands of years of habitation, a cultural landscape of remarkable complexity and depth. As others have pointed out, wildness (still more than beauty) depends on the eye of the beholder.

Lesley Macinnes presents the view as seen from the desk of Historic Scotland, seeking 'to ensure that succeeding generations inherit a landscape which physically connects the past with the present'. It is a good vision: embracing both continuity and change, while retaining characteristics from the past with which people can connect. It involves recognising the fluid nature of the boundaries between the natural and cultural, honouring local distinctiveness and putting in the foreground one all-important fact: the past belongs to everyone and can be learnt from by everyone. This is surely an important statement of intent from an agency seeing the need to be outgoing and proactive, and tuned to the political as well as the cultural and academic needs of a new century.

To counterbalance, and to bring us back to the reality of what the picture might look like from the other end of the telescope, Jean Balfour argues the case of the landowner and farmer working in the difficult economic and political environment of the modern countryside. The landowner, the farmer and the crofter, she argues, have basically learned to live with nature conservation and scenic designations, but find different and perhaps more difficult problems from archaeology. One aspect is the enormous number of unscheduled sites, vastly more than anyone, save specialist archaeologists, are at all aware. Another aspect is external confusion in perceiving 'who has the last word' in archaeological conservation. There is no undercurrent of public opinion emphasising why archaeology in general is important, as there is with nature conservation and scenic protection. There is no clear popular understanding of which bits of archaeology in particular are important. The owners of the sites, therefore, often feel resentful of proposed restrictions. Whether such observations are justified or not from the perspective of Historic Scotland, it is important to know that out on the ground there are some who see their procedures as either insufficiently comprehensive or insufficiently selective, and their priorities and choices as sometimes unclear.

Caroline Earwood invites us to lift our heads from Scotland and explore the Welsh experience on Forest Enterprise land, explaining how archaeological survey is proceeding using GIS (Geographical Information System) as a key tool. A key problem affecting all our uplands is that of achieving 'protection of archaeological sites and landscapes within the day-to-day management of the forest', and the systematic and comprehensive co-operation between Welsh archaeologists and foresters form a practical model for us all. A different aspect of work-in-progress was demonstrated by Jack Stevenson and Lynn Dyson Bruce, who described the RCAHMS project to map the multi-layered character of the historic landscape. As they say, 'modern landscape itself is an archaeological monument', and in this context archaeology is not so much a closely defined discipline as a series of techniques designed to describe historical geography, the 'interplay between the natural and man-made environment'. The illustrations for this book come from their splendid series of maps, showing how RCAHMS is uncovering the texture of the historical landscape in its natural setting.

The last two chapters are devoted to the collaboration of scientists and historians or archaeologists. Richard Hingley and Hugh Ingram, in a carefully worked study of the ecological and historical aspects of peat bogs, argue that they can only be understood within a cultural context. Bogs arose in their present form in Scotland probably through a combination of natural and anthropomorphic factors, and were maintained over generations by human intervention, including a light level of burning and of grazing by domestic stock. All the well-meaning conservation in the world may come to nothing unless we take account of this and accordingly glean from the past those features of human management that tended towards the bogs' preservation. In conserving a peat bog, the authors remind us, we preserve an archive of human activity in the plant remains just as surely as we preserve a habitat of nature.

In the final contribution, Alan Hampson and myself urge the need for collaboration between forestry and history to improve our understanding of woodland and its present and future management in the landscape. Woods, like bogs, cannot be seen apart from their history of exploitation through millennia, a process that has shaped their character and their value in natural, cultural and economic terms. Any modern decision on how to manage a wood is itself cultural, involving a range of human aims and values. The survival of ancient woodland in an age of democratic decision-making can best be assured by satisfying a range of objectives with which the public can identify – the production of timber, the protection of biodiversity and archaeology, and the provision of recreation are all normally compatible. The task for the historian is to get both public and scientific opinion to realise how a wood is a piece of history as well as a piece of ecology and forestry.

Many obligations are incurred in the production of a book of this kind, not least to the other participants in the seminar whose observations and comments often encouraged the authors of papers to look at their contributions afresh. The largest debts, however, are to Historic Scotland for a subvention that made publication possible, to the Royal Commission on the Ancient and Historical Monuments of Scotland for subsidising the production of the colour plates, and to Scottish Natural Heritage for allowing us the venue without charge. To all we are very grateful.

T. C. Smout
Centre for Environmental History and Policy
Universities of St Andrews and Stirling

1

The Northern Landscape Yesterday, Today and Tomorrow

R. J. MERCER

'Kinraddie lands had been won by a Norman childe, Cospatric de Gondeshil, in the days of William the Lyon, when gryphons and such-like beasts still roamed the Scots countryside and folk would waken in their beds to hear the children screaming, with a great wolf-beast, come through the hide window, tearing at their throats. In the Den of Kinraddie one such beast had its lair and by day it lay about the woods and the stench of it was awful to smell . . . '

Lewis Grassic Gibbon *Sunset Song* (1932), Prelude

'Landscape' is a word of comparatively short pedigree in our language. First registered by the *Shorter Oxford Dictionary* as of the very end of the sixteenth century, it is a Dutch export to these islands – the Dutch word *'landskip'* serving to distinguish terrestrial from marine studies of nature conducted in two dimensions, usually in oil paint, relating the endless variety of Man's relationships with nature and its relationships with him. From the outset, then, the word 'landscape' relates to an artefact, indeed, an artifice.

The science of landscape painting appears to have emerged in northern Europe in the early sixteenth century, notable originators being the painters Mathias Grünewald (1460–1527, whose actual name was probably Mathias Neithart), who worked in the little town of Seligenstadt, near Frankfurt, and Albrecht Altdorfer (1485–1538) who, working in Regensburg with Lucas Cranach (1472–1553) shared this unusual interest in landscape portrayal. Kenneth Clark classified these early experimenters as 'original expressionists' (Clark, 1949, 51), founding a northern tradition of singular longevity which, by way of Turner (1775–1851), led directly to Van Gogh (1853–1890) and Munch (1863–1944). Grünewald's wonderful *Isenheim altarpiece* (c.1512–16, now in the Musée d' Unterlinden, Colmar, France) sets the Temptation of St Anthony and his meeting with St Paul the Hermit in the wilderness; a moment of great torment set against a fearful background of mountain and forest – the first such depiction in North European art. Altdorfer, in his extraordinary painting of *Susannah Bathing* (1526, now in the Alte Pinakothek, Munich), represents an enclosed palace garden in which events take place with the mountain and forest wilderness austere and imprisoning without. In the same gallery Lucas Cranach shows in his *Golden Age* healthy, naked humans dancing as animals graze in a garden full of fruit and flowers, while beyond a high wall spans the entire picture, and mountain crag and forest form a forbidding backcloth.

It is no coincidence that Grünewald earned his living not only as a painter of genius but also as an hydrographic engineer and architect-cum-landscape gardener for the Archbishops of Mainz. His appreciation of the shape and lie of the land must have been a profound one and we shall return, briefly, to the development of *designed* landscape in due course. It is, however, interesting to find designed landscape and depicted landscape united in one genius at this early stage.

At this point it is apposite to introduce the contrast between the northern landscape record and its southern counterpart. Born in Umbria between 1410 and 1420, Piero della Francesca absorbed the colossal technical advances in the creation of the illusion of light and in the mathematical calculation of perspective that had been developed in Florence by the middle of the fifteenth century. He combined these advances in a way that renders him probably the greatest painter of landscape in fifteenth-century Italy and his work at its summit can be seen in the background of his portraits of the Duke and Duchess of Urbino (*c.*1465, in the Uffizi Gallery, Florence) and in both of his altarpieces in the National Gallery, London (*The Baptism*, 1442, and *The Nativity*, *c.*1472). But the contrast with the north is total – the landscape is not distanced, it is bathed in the same light as the foreground and it is 'domesticated' it is the highly integrated landscape that surrounded and supported the city states of Northern Italy.

In sum, *landskip* is an artefact, a contrivance, created to allow the expression of the multifarious aspects of the relationship between human beings and the natural world of which they are a part. In Europe, this invention took place no earlier than the fifteenth century and immediately assumed the character of a vibrant counterpoint between North and South where, in Northern Europe, an 'expressionist' approach developed that allowed the tension between Man and the mountain and forest of the North European Plain and its southern margin to be released. Southern painters had looked longer on landscapes, surrounding the towns of Tuscany, Umbria and North Italy with greater composure and, perhaps in thrall to the humanist focus of their Renaissance, showing, generally, a more domesticated landscape.

The word 'domesticated' has been carefully chosen. Today we would, perhaps, view the landscape of the vast majority of Europe as a gigantic witness to Man's emergent dominance – his domestication of the animals, plants and topography that surround him. But, as with all animals, where domestication is the genetic eradication of the fear of Man, so at another level the landscape and our response to it is a witness to Man's own domestication – his own conquest of the fear of his surroundings; his rejection of his isolation within enclaves of established control.

Just as farming itself, therefore, arrived upon the coastal forelands of the Mediterranean about three thousand years before it was established in Britain and the north, so other forms of landscape understanding and appreciation also took some time to permeate what was, nevertheless, a two-way membrane. The neuroses that, as reality or metaphor, myth or philosophy, characterised the North European vision of man's surroundings refer back to forest, mountain, moor and river, and the fear that has been generated there in the hearts of urban populations. Those born in familiarity with the woods mires and mountains, of course, felt no qualms, no fundamental and illogical threat; they were part of that environment. Any superficial examination of Celtic poetry of the medieval period will demonstrate this to be the case (see, for example, 'The Cliff of Alternan' (Jackson 1971, 180) composed probably in Co. Sligo in the twelfth century).

But history is usually written by the victor, and the historian has been an urban creature, always wary of the uncontrolled and largely undocumented. It is, therefore, unsurprising that the urban view, dominant in terms of both patronage and execution, should create 'landskip' as an urban-inspired art, and that its development should be taken over by that most urbanised of north European communities in the Low Countries, where not only were urbanised perceptions dominant but, perhaps to a unique extent in Europe, the countryside was a creation of Man himself.

By the later sixteenth century the portrayal of a culturally determined landscape was to dominate the artistic horizon in Europe, whether in realistic or idealised form. Peter Paul Rubens (1577–1640) provided a bridge between the externalised landscape of Altdorfer and the domesticated landscape of the seventeenth century. The realistic vision of artists like Hobbema (1638–1709) and Jacob van Ruisdael (1628–1682), conveyed a vision of Nature which, while harking back to the expressionism of the early sixteenth century, also looks forward to the resolution of the tension between northern and southern vision of landscape, as exemplified by the work of Claude Lorraine (1600–1682) and by the English painters, notably Constable (1776–1837), in the late eighteenth century.

The later years of the sixteenth century saw not only the beginning of the endeavour to portray landscape itself as a cultural artefact but also the attempt to create it as an aesthetic ideal. Medieval emparkment had been, if anything, an endeavour to preserve wilderness within the increasingly domesticated landscape of the high Medieval period. The Renaissance saw the movement to create an idealised landscape as cultivated artefact, excluding both wilderness and the 'economic' landscape of farming and production. This process, following variant fashions of formality, romanticism and utilitarian ideals, has continued until the present day, first as formal grounds now (interestingly) being recreated at sites (for example, Het Loo and Hampton Court) across Europe, then, after the middle of the eighteenth century, with contrived romantic 'wildness' (now being conserved but *not* recreated) and then the High Victorian urban recreation areas of the urban parks of our great cities.

One other area of intellectual and perceptional development which reflects upon the emergence of the modern concept of landscape was created, again in the sixteenth century, in the science of mapping (as opposed to portrayal of geographies). This was an attempt to present an holistic view of landscape, reflecting the various economic, aesthetic and physical components of 'the landscape' in an inclusive, non-externalising way. This science (only now being revolutionised by the ability to create the 'infinite' maps of the Geographical Information System as opposed to the 'finite' paper map) was based in two complementary needs. One was the increasing integration of landscape-use and economy, whereby conflicting and supplementary policies had to be weighed against one another, as, of course, they still do. Economic and social crowding demanded, and still demands, mapping. The other was 'policy pursued by other means' and the development of military organisation and strategy, and the new 'Machiavellian' policy-realism of the humanist revolution required the widest possible canvas upon which to exercise itself. The military world of manoeuvre for advantage to battle-climax, as opposed to agreed and pre-recognised formal battle-climax, required geo-spatial precision and landscape appreciation hitherto unknown.

So much, then, for the complexity of the origins of our perception of landscape and of the different origins of that perception – geographical, intellectual, economic, social, military and aesthetic. Perhaps now we must return to 'the north-south divide' and examine the psychological origins of our modern perception. Simon Schama (1995) contrasts what he calls 'the northern landscape myth', wherein the wilderness of forest, mire and river still exercises a powerful, perhaps subliminal, contrast, with 'La douce France' which:

describes as much a geography as a history, the sweetness of a classically well-ordered place where rivers, cultivated fields, orchards, vineyards and woods are all in harmonious balance with one another.

Within this historico-geographic model, established less than 500 years ago, lies the origin of another dynamic and still current force (of unknown and unpredictable potential) – patriotism – which also emerges as another component of the Pandora's box that was opened in northern Europe in the later sixteenth century.

Since the 1750s, landscape development has been a relatively fully documented and witnessed feature of British history. Economic pressure has led to massive depopulation and urban concentration in all parts of this crowded island and the recognition of landscape change as a result had become the currency of commentators from Thomas More and Spenser onwards. Only in one broad area of the island did the shift in sociology and perception not meet an equivalent change in economic focus and technological advance. Not in Cornwall, nor in the Pennine area, nor in Northumberland; not in Central or even Southern Scotland; only in the Highland areas of Scotland was the demolition of the old order, accompanied by little pre-structured aesthetic, intellectual or technological order, urban-developed. The result was a compromise resting between wilderness *simpliciter* and the development of a wilderness of leisure, the potential for the limitless provision of which was created by the co-existing but geographically divorced Industrial Revolution. Such a reality was conjured in an atmosphere of a Romantic endeavour to foster Man's awe of a Nature untamed, a juxtaposition of forces that created the artificial and unstable inheritance that exists in Highland Scotland today, quite foreign to the dynamic processes of the preceding four to five thousand years.

The power of nineteenth-century inspired aesthetic, social, economic and intellectual traditions is not to be underestimated, and the writer suggests that, perhaps again subliminally, they dominate our landscape (and indeed townscape) perceptions today. Popular perception of the Scottish landscape is closer to Landseer's (1802–1873) vision and to the images of Sir Walter Scott as best developed in *Rob Roy* (published in 1817) – paradoxically, the latter archetype having long disappeared to make way for the hunting scenes of the former – than it is to any intellectualised construct of today. Bearing in mind comments drawn from Schama, we may challenge these deeply held perceptions, and their baggage-train of political, patriotic and psychological forces, at our peril.

Into this *imbroglio* field archaeology has stepped, like a two-year-old into Princes Street. With techniques only seriously developed since the 1960s, it has begun (largely through the work of the RCAHMS) to reconstruct the reality of the historic and prehistoric Scottish landscape in all its complexity, variety and time-depth. To create a landscape register, multi-layered, inclusive and multiply articulated, will be the work of decades. To do this RCAHMS has already developed its Geographical Information System to allow the multi-layering and multiple articulation of data. It has also, with Historic Scotland and in partnership with other bodies (SNH and the Forestry Commission), embarked upon a range of programmes which will be described in a paper by Jack Stevenson at Chapter 6.

In drawing together the strands of this brief but very wide-ranging and, the writer hopes, provocative discussion, the following points should perhaps be emphasised:

1) In Europe any coherent view of 'landscape', 'scenic value', 'the interrelationship of Man and the landscape' and his perception of it, only began to emerge at the end of the fifteenth century – a mere five hundred years ago.

2) The fruit of that perception has always been an artefact and an artifice very largely generated by urban-based intellectual forces, reflecting in the northern context a range of complex psychological issues.

3) Through time, a broadening range of interests, among them social, aesthetic, economic, military, recreational and political, have all, without any inter-communication, added their own emphases.

4) The landscape and its mythology have exerted profound influences upon our self perception, our developing politics and sense of patriotism and our material and intellectual culture. Schama argues convincingly that deep psychological divisions exist between his 'northern' perception (to which the writer would ally Scotland) and 'la douce France' (and perhaps southern England).

5) Current popular perceptions of the Scottish landscape, notably in the urban context, tend to be founded in perceptions developed during the high Romantic period of the early and middle nineteenth century in spite of the frequent lack of any internal consistency.

6) Landscape field archaeology, the essential 'handmaid of history' in the relatively thin oxygen (documentarily speaking) of the rural landscape is a very young science – younger (and hugely less well resourced!) than rocket science or nuclear fission. It is perhaps ironic that the study of our actual landscape history and its actual progression lags far behind, in developmental terms, our study of our universe and our distant origins. Good progress is

being made, however, with RCAHMS often in pilot position, although a great deal remains to be done.

We now enter a period, it is generally agreed, of potentially great landscape change in Scotland. The writer hopes that this paper has indicated that there are no 'inherited certainties' in the debate which must follow, and that that debate *must* be inclusive. The 'landscape', the perception of 'scenic quality', the definition of 'beauty', 'quality', 'heritage' and 'importance' are founded in a quagmire of inherited and often unquestioned assumptions, arrived at quite accidentally, through a range of media (aesthetic, historical, social and political) with relatively little overarching consideration or thought. Politicians, patriots, ecologists, historical archaeologists, soldiers, farmers, foresters, urban dwellers – all of us – must be drawn to the consideration of 'where we have been' and then, perhaps, 'where do we go now'.

REFERENCES

Clark, K. (1949). *Landscape into Art*. London, John Murray.
Jackson, K. H. (1971). *A Celtic Miscellany* (revised edition). Harmondsworth.
Schama, S. (1995). *Landscape and Memory*. London, Harper Collins.

2

The Historic Landscape in Scotland: Towards a Strategy for the Future

LESLEY MACINNES

BACKGROUND

There are established and well-documented policies in place for the conservation of the built heritage within both central and local government (Hunter and Ralston, 1993). In Scotland, the built heritage is widely defined to encompass ancient monuments and archaeological sites and landscapes; historic buildings, parks and gardens; designed landscapes; and historic townscapes (HS 1994,4; NPPG 18, para. 1). Ancient monuments and archaeological sites are protected under the Ancient Monuments and Archaeological Areas Act, 1979, which allows for monuments to be taken into guardianship by the State (usually known as 'Properties in Care') or the local authority, and for the protection of nationally important monuments called 'Scheduled Ancient Monuments' (Breeze, 1993, 4450; NPPG 5). Historic buildings and areas are protected under the Town and Country Planning (Scotland) Act, 1997, as Listed Buildings, which are sub-divided into three categories of significance, and Conservation Areas (HS 1998a; NPPG 18). Also relevant is the World Heritage Convention, which seeks to protect cultural and natural sites of outstanding universal significance. At present, 'Edinburgh Old and New Towns' and 'The Heart of Neolithic Orkney' are the only sites in Scotland inscribed on the World Heritage List on cultural grounds. The selection criteria for protection under these main designations have been set down clearly elsewhere (Breeze, 1993, 4446; AMBS 1983; HS 1998a; Prott, 1992, 6769).

There are further provisions for the conservation of the historic environment within the planning system. Protection of the built heritage is recognised as a material consideration in the planning process, mainly through Structure and Local Plans supported by development control procedures. The focus of these provisions can extend beyond individual buildings and monuments to protect landscape areas, including sites on the non-statutory *Inventory of Historic Gardens and Designed Landscapes*; townscapes and urban archaeology; and the setting of buildings or monuments, whether or not they are scheduled or listed. In addition, local authorities can designate areas of special significance for the cultural heritage within their locality. *National Planning Policy Guideline 5 (Archaeology and Planning), Planning Advice Note 42 (Archaeology: the Planning Process and Scheduled Monument Procedures)* and *National Planning Policy Guideline 18 (Planning and the Historic Environment)* provide convenient summaries of the role of the planning process in the protection of the historic environment in Scotland.

The main focus of current provisions for protection and management is on individual sites or discrete heritage areas, albeit at times fairly extensive (Breeze, 1993; Macinnes, 1993a). They all present problems in relation to the conservation of the wider historic landscape. Overall, the system depends on the state of knowledge about types of sites, and it requires clear definition of areas to be protected. Some types of site, especially more modern features, pose particular problems. Some survive in great numbers and cover extensive areas, such as Medieval or Later Rural Settlement (Hingley, 1993); others are overlain by deep deposits, as with stratified urban features (for example, Holdsworth, 1987, 210-212; Dennison and Stones, 1997, 31) and peatlands (Hingley *et al.*, 1999), while others have particularly significant local variations, like vernacular farm buildings (for example, Brunskill, 1987; Naismith, 1985). For such sites, selection criteria for protection have to be particularly rigorous and transparent to the non-specialist as, on the one hand, their very ubiquity can appear to make them less valuable (though in many ways this enhances their archaeological value), while, on the other hand, their protection has greater impact on the management and development of the modern landscape. Initiatives are in place to address such problems and identify the most suitable candidates for protection under existing provisions (for example, HS, 1998b; Owen, 1999). Nevertheless, it is also clear that the scope of some types of sites is so extensive that their conservation needs to be considered within a strategy for the landscape as a whole, rather than on a site by site basis. In general, the historic character of the wider Scottish environment, whether rural or urban, is neither well understood nor adequately considered in the predominantly site-specific focus of existing conservation mechanisms. Broader landscape designations, such as National Scenic Areas, do not generally give significant consideration to the historic dimension of landscape, though some could do so in principle (*cf.* Miles,

1992, 103), and may do so in future (*cf.* SNH, 1998 and 1999).

The importance of the wider environment in sustaining modern life and in maintaining biodiversity and cultural diversity is now widely acknowledged (see, for example, the suite of Government documents *This Common Inheritance,* 1990; *Sustainable Development Strategy,* 1994; *Biodiversity UK Action Plan,* 1994; *Opportunities for Change,* 1998; *Down to Earth,* 1998). Similarly, the conservation of the built heritage is beginning to be set within this broader framework, and the historic nature of the wider landscape, as opposed to select areas, is beginning to be acknowledged (for example, Darvill *et al.,* 1993; Jacques, 1995; Rossler, 1995; Dyson Bruce *et al.,* 1999; Herring, 1998). This development is to be welcomed, but it requires cultural resource managers to move away from the past focus on individual sites to a landscape-based approach, and this presents difficult challenges in the fields of recording, protection, management and interpretation.

Against this background, this paper seeks to clarify Historic Scotland's vision for the future of Scotland's historic landscape, and to outline the strategies that are beginning to be developed for its protection and management in the twenty-first century.

INTRODUCTION

Historic Scotland's strategy for the historic landscape is guided by three principles. The first is HS's own Mission Statement, to 'safeguard the nation's built heritage and promote its understanding and enjoyment'. Secondly, we seek to develop the links between these aims of protection, understanding and enjoyment, building on the idea that 'through interpretation, understanding; through understanding, appreciation; through appreciation, protection' (Tilden, 1957). Finally, we seek to embrace the principles of sustainability, following the Council for British Archaeology's definition of sustainable development in relation to the historic environment: 'development which meets the needs of today without compromising the ability of future generations to understand, appreciate and benefit from Britain's historic environment' (Clark, 1993, 90).

In applying these principles to the historic landscape, we are seeking to promote understanding and awareness of the historic development of the modern landscape; and to secure the conservation of key elements for the benefit of present and future generations. We are pursuing these aims within the context of land-use planning, land management and wider environmental conservation, recognising that the historical dimension is only one of the multiple facets of the Scottish landscape.

In outlining Historic Scotland's vision for the historic landscape in the next century, and the strategic objectives needed to realise it, we fully acknowledge that other bodies have a role to play in bringing this vision to reality. We also recognise that others have their own visions for the historic landscape. Therefore, this paper is not intended to be prescriptive, but rather to achieve recognition of the historical depth of the Scottish landscape and to stimulate discussion of the implications of this for management of the landscape in future.

THE VISION

In summary, Historic Scotland seeks to ensure that succeeding generations inherit a landscape which physically connects the past with the present, and which retains sufficient threads of the past to enable its broad history to be interpreted (cf. Atkinson, 1995, 4). It is our vision that the landscape of the future – and its management – will have the following range of characteristics:

A landscape that is historically rich and retains visible characteristics of its past

The historic landscape is an integral part of the modern environment, and provides evidence of real time-depth (Macinnes and Wickham-Jones, 1992). It is made up of elements of the tangible built heritage – ancient monuments and archaeological sites and landscapes; historic buildings; parks and gardens; and designed landscapes. Features occur variously in rural, urban, marine and underwater contexts. These various components of the historic landscape range in date from the earliest human activity some 10,000 years ago to the present day, covering all aspects of human activity. Some are clearly visible, some visible only to the trained eye, and some known only through specialist techniques such as air photography, geophysics or palaeobotany. The historic landscape also encompasses the wider setting of these features, and the inter-relationships that turn individual sites into landscapes (cf. Darvill *et al.*, 1993, 565). It further includes the less tangible historical, artistic and literary associations of place (for useful discussion, see Muir, 1999). It has, therefore, both an objective resource base, which is recorded in a variety of databases, most notably the national and local sites and monuments records, and a more subjective quality or sense of place which is less easy to define, but which is, nonetheless, important. HS's vision is to ensure that the landscape maintains its remarkable time-depth and associated historic characteristics into the future.

A dynamic landscape which embraces both continuity and change

Though the historic elements of the landscape are themselves finite, they constitute, at the same time, a dynamic resource which grows and alters with time. The landscape itself bears witness to the tension between continuity on the one hand, and the constant process of change on the other. A modern approach to the historic landscape needs to embrace both states. Nevertheless, the twentieth century has seen such a dramatic rate of change through intensive human activity that HS believes it is now important to redress the balance by focusing on managed evolution at a more measured pace. Our aim is to help manage the process of change in a way which is more conscious, more informed and more historically aware than has generally been the case in the past.

An approach to landscape which embraces both its cultural and natural aspects and seeks to integrate these in decision-making and management

An historical view of landscape clearly indicates that the boundaries between its natural and cultural elements are not static, but rather fluid and closely interwoven (see Muir, 1999, *passim*). Indeed, studies of modern primitive societies demonstrate that divisions between cultural and natural perspectives of landscape are very largely a western cultural construct (*cf.* McNeely and Keeton, 1995). Nevertheless, we live in a country where ownership of the landscape is extensive, and responsibility for it compartmentalised, and this has a major impact on landscape policy and conservation practice (Callander, 1998; Callander and Wightman, 1998). In practice, there is a close relationship between the management of landscape for its cultural and natural interest (Berry and Brown, 1995, *passim*), yet it can be difficult to manage the landscape holistically, recognising its underlying unity and the common ground within our sectoral approaches to it. HS's vision for the future, therefore, is to promote closer integration of the cultural and natural aspects of landscape in the process of both decision-making and practical management.

Recognition and celebration of the cultural diversity within the landscape, and wider participation in its conservation and management

Conservation of the historic landscape in the UK has traditionally been top-down, highly specialised and focused on nationally important features and national priorities. For the future, we need to find more ways to honour the common-place and locally distinctive features which form the basic fabric of our historic environment. We should seek to foster pride in the great diversity within the historic landscape, recognising that this represents the different histories of different communities: this has, perhaps, particular resonance as Scotland seeks to re-affirm its national identity in the wake of the new Parliament. Many local and representative groups already have a keen interest in their local cultural heritage, as indeed do many land owners and occupiers who play a key role in the management of the historic landscape (*cf.* Iles, 1992, 1359). But we need to engage their interest more and encourage greater involvement if we are to ensure that the landscape retains its historic diversity into the future.

A landscape that enriches society and provides a source of knowledge and understanding, inspiration and enjoyment

The archaeological and historic landscape is studied predominantly by academics of various disciplines (see, for example, Aalen, 1996), while its management, at both national and local level, is led by specialists (for example, Hunter and Ralston, 1993). But the past belongs to everyone, and a wide range of people are interested in its physical remains, whether they are our great archaeological and architectural jewels or small features of particular local interest. Although public access and enjoyment has always been an important aspect of national policy – as, indeed, is evident from Historic Scotland's Mission Statement – HS's vision for the future is to widen people's engagement with the historic landscape, and to foster the innate interest people have in the past of their local landscape by facilitating the excitement of discovery, the processes of learning and understanding, and participation in conservation and interpretation. If protection does indeed stem from understanding and appreciation, then this aim is highly important if we are to sustain the historic characteristics of the landscape into the future.

A forum for education

People can learn about the historic landscape, and they can learn from the historic landscape. It is of vital importance to our understanding of all periods and all aspects of the past, and its component parts form a primary resource for study. It is of value not only to specialists within a wide variety of disciplines (for example, Aalen, 1996, 15–102), but also for general education where students can be introduced to a variety of subjects (such as, archaeology, architectural history, ecology, geology, botany) and a wide array of investigative techniques. From the historic landscape we can also learn lessons from the past which have value to society in a number of ways, particularly relating to our varied but inextricable relationship with our natural environment (*cf.* Barber and Welsh, 1992). This is an area with particular scope for further development and creativity in the future.

STRATEGIC OBJECTIVES

To help achieve this vision for the historic landscape, Historic Scotland has identified a number of strategic objectives, listed below. Other key objectives will undoubtedly be identified in the course of further discussions with a range of partners.

Enhanced recognition and understanding of the historic landscape through recording, research and investigation

To this end, HS considers it important to encourage and support resource audits of the historic landscape, and relevant research linked to strategic aims and objectives. There is a good existing base on which to build for the future. Particular note might be made of the range of landscape survey work undertaken by the Royal Commission on the Ancient and Historical Monuments of Scotland (RCAHMS), both in the field (for example, RCAHMS, 1990; 1994; 1997; 1998) and desk-based (for example, the First Edition Survey Project); area-based resource audits linked to national priorities, such as the Cairngorm Partnership Area and the proposed National Park for Loch Lomond and the Trossachs; and the farm-based conservation audits required under the agri-environmental schemes. Other field-based projects, such as the Upper Clyde Valley Landscape Project (DES, 1998, 79 and 89) and the National Trust for Scotland's Ben Lawers Project (DES, 1998, 75), are investigating the development of the landscape and considering aspects of conservation. All of these will contribute considerably to our understanding of the historic landscape and its conservation needs. Thematic projects are also extremely valuable in addressing particular problems, such as Medieval or Later Rural Settlement or the Military Defence of Britain. Research into particular conservation problems, like coastal erosion (Ashmore, 1994) or the effect of vegetation and burrowing animals (Dunwell and Trout, 1999), is also crucial.

While these approaches will continue to develop, two initiatives seem particularly promising for their potential to clarify the nature and development of Scotland's historic landscape. Firstly, there is the recent development of a technique for assessing the historic landscape, Historic Landuse Assessment (HLA), which complements and adds historical depth to the more established technique of Landscape Character Assessment (Dyson Bruce *et al.*, 1999, 12). Following a series of pilots, HLA has already been undertaken for nearly twenty per cent of the country. It should prove an important tool for defining the regional characteristics of the historic landscape and, thereby, the cultural diversity of the landscape as a whole; it will help provide overviews of the development of the landscape over time at both the national and regional level; it can inform planning and land-use strategies; and it can guide more detailed work (Dyson Bruce, *op. cit.*, 71–8).

The second initiative is the Scottish Burgh Survey, which identifies the nature of the archaeological resource in our historic burghs and urban areas in order to inform decision-making for planning, development control, protection and management (for example, Dennison and Coleman, 1998; *cf.* Murray, 1983). This series provides vital information for the most populated areas of Scotland, and complements the rural focus of the HLA. Together, these new approaches will move us gradually away from the past focus on individual sites and monuments and give us a much clearer understanding of the nature and development of the historic environment in Scotland on which to base future conservation and research strategies.

Protection and management of the historic characteristics of landscape based on informed and integrated decision making

The improvements in our knowledge-base consequent on the above will undoubtedly aid strategic decision-making for planning, land-management and cultural resource management. This should in turn improve prioritisation of objectives for protection and management, such as within the scheduling programme and the agri-environment schemes, allowing these to be targeted more effectively towards important historic landscape issues. This broader view will complement the statutory protection, largely site-based, of specific historic and archaeological features and identify the need for any historic landscape designation in future. It will also highlight the relationship between the historic landscape and other landscape interests, and inform other designations which impact on the historic landscape (*cf.* Lambrick, 1992; SNH, 1998 and 1999).

Indeed, it is important that enhanced understanding of the characteristics of the historic landscape, and of national and regional diversity, be combined with approaches in related fields, particularly Scottish Natural Heritage's Landscape Character Assessments and Natural Heritage Zones, to facilitate better informed and more integrated strategies for town and country planning and land-use management. A more integrated approach to landscape management will not only provide a clearer understanding of the range of values attributed to the modern landscape and the concomitant range of management options, but it will also help to reduce the potential for conflict, thereby helping to maximise the benefit for the landscape as a whole (see Countryside Commission *et al.*, 1997).

Wider recognition of the diversity within the historic landscape, particularly its regional and local value

Scheduling and listing provide statutory recognition for nationally important features. To some extent local importance is also recognised in protective measures through the listing process and in conservation areas, as well as more generally within the planning system through structure and local plan policies. However, more emphasis needs to be placed on characterising the whole of the historic landscape, and on recognising local importance and the value of undesignated elements within the landscape. Trends and initiatives mentioned earlier will undoubtedly assist in this, particularly HLA and the Scottish Burgh Survey, together with a more integrated approach to planning and land management. Nevertheless, further work is needed to identify and address local priorities within both the planning system and land management schemes; and to encompass within them local landscape elements, such as farm buildings and stone dykes, which have high visibility and generate local interest but which have not attracted much study in the past. Designed landscapes, which have had a major aesthetic impact on the landscape, also deserve closer attention, though they present significant problems as they cover large areas under diverse management and often in multiple ownership. Similarly, remains of Medieval or Later Rural Settlement need to be acknowledged as important landscape elements; though these survive in great numbers, they display considerable regional and local variation, and are often well-known locally (*cf.* Mackay, 1993, 489). Recognising that such issues are likely to be of great concern at local level, HS aims to provide support by seeking to build consideration of such features into national management schemes and systems of designation when the opportunity arises, as, for example, with the establishment of National Parks and the review of National Scenic Areas. Indeed, we regard it as highly important that any modern landscape designation should not only combine natural and cultural elements, but should also balance both national and local priorities.

Encouragement of interpretation, access and sustainable tourism

Although elements of the historic landscape can be vulnerable to damage from visitors, this problem can usually be managed and most features can survive a reasonable amount of visiting provided good practice is followed (for example, Breeze, 1994). HS wishes to encourage and support greater public understanding and enjoyment of the range of historic landscape features and their wider environmental context. This may be through formal presentation schemes or involve minimal interpretation, allowing the personal process of discovery to take place. We aim to support access and interpretation initiatives through appropriate grant schemes, including the agri-environment schemes, and by ensuring that all policy developments relating to access consider the place of the cultural heritage. Again, there are important current initiatives to build on, most notably Tourism Management Schemes and the Council for Scottish Archaeology's Adopt-a-Monument Scheme, both of which involve the important principles of partnership and community participation, and present good models for the future (see *Tourism and the Scottish Environment: A Sustainable Partnership,* undated). These initiatives also emphasise the link between conservation and interpretation, while the partnership approach of Tourism Management Schemes in particular usually has the significant added value of promoting the integration of different landscape elements. There are also an increasing number of exciting private initiatives with a significant educational content, such as Archaeolink, the Loch Tay Crannog and the Kilmartin House Centre for Archaeology and Landscape Interpretation. To help maintain high standards, some of the relevant public agencies, including HS, are actively developing guidance on principles and best practice in interpretation and sustainable tourism through Interpret Scotland, and through the Tourism and Environment Forum. Although there is a wide range of organisations involved in the field of landscape interpretation, the role played by agencies and local authorities in setting standards, and in demonstrating good practice through the various properties in public care, is likely to remain important in the future (see, for example, SNH, 1997).

Dissemination of knowledge and education

An important objective is to ensure that public records relating to the historic landscape are easily accessible to the public in a user-friendly form, wherever possible from local bases. Since existing records are highly specialised, this must be something of a long-term aim and can only be achieved with the full involvement of local partners. However, some important steps have already been taken in this direction. Most significant is RCAHMS' CANMORE web-system for public access to the National Monuments Record of Scotland (NMRS). Another important development is the Scottish Cultural Resource Access Network (SCRAN), which aims to facilitate local computerised access to a wide range of data relating to the historic landscape and cultural heritage. There is also an increased emphasis on the use of the historic landscape as a prime educational resource at all levels, as in the examples mentioned in the previous paragraph. These innovative centres combine interpretative displays with practical and experimental approaches to capture the imagination of school-children and the general public. More traditional approaches remain important, however, such as the work of in-house education officers with school-children, as within Historic Scotland itself. Similarly, publications which aim to make aspects of Scotland's history and prehistory more accessible can be both useful and successful, as witnessed by the numerous guidebooks available and the recent collaborative series between HS and Batsford or Canongate. Yet there is always room for more educational work, and good quality initiatives should be actively encouraged, not only towards including the study of the historic landscape in mainstream and environmental education, but also in support of inter-disciplinary and locally-based schemes.

Applying the principles of sustainable development to the historic landscape, including greater public participation

With the widespread adoption of sustainable development as a framework for decision-making, it is vital that consideration be given to the problem of how to apply the principle of sustainability to the historic environment. This process may gradually move us away from the current highly specialised and professional view of the landscape to one which embraces a wider range of perspectives. It is important that we learn to demonstrate the value of the historic landscape more clearly to society, making more transparent its role in understanding the past; in contributing to landscape, ecological and cultural diversity; in providing an important economic, recreational and educational resource; and in offering a rich source of enjoyment and inspiration. Such values need to be recognised within the framework of sustainable development, particularly as they relate to each of its three principal aspects – social, economic and environmental well-being. It is further important to encourage wider public participation in research, conservation and interpretation of the historic landscape.

Some steps are already being taken towards addressing these general issues and providing guidelines for the sustainable use of the historic landscape. Notable initiatives have been the Stirling Charter: Conserving Scotland's Built Heritage; and the Duthchas Project, which explored local public participation in the context of sustainable development in three pilot areas in Highland and the Western Isles. Building on this experience, and relevant work elsewhere in the UK (especially Countryside Commission *et al.*, 1996 and 1997; English Heritage, 1997), HS is preparing a statement on the sustainable use of the historic environment, which we hope will ultimately help guide us all towards its more sensitive use for the benefit of both present and future generations.

Ensure that historic landscapes, and an integrated approach to landscape management, are properly embraced within UK, European and international provisions and associated organisational structures

We need to exert greater influence on national and international initiatives and directives relating to the cultural landscape. A significant problem here is the compartmentalisation of both national and European organisational structures which sometimes appears to militate against the comprehensive inclusion of cultural heritage in environmental initiatives on the one hand, and against the integration of cultural and natural aspects of landscape planning and management on the other (*cf.* Macinnes, 1993b, 102).

At a national level these problems have been ameliorated to some extent by the Statement of Intent between Historic Scotland and Scottish Natural Heritage, which has led to improved collaboration on landscape matters (HS and SNH, 1995). Outside the national agencies, the improvement of archaeological representation on bodies such as Scottish Environment Link, and the John Muir Trust has been vitally important in integrating approaches to landscape among key voluntary organisations, with a consequent influence on the development of national landscape policy.

There has also been progress within land management, witnessed by the Forestry Commission's recent *UK Forestry Standard* (1998) and the revision of the agri-environment schemes. National Parks, which address cultural heritage issues as well as natural heritage and which, founded on the principle of sustainable development, should become a significant model for integrated land management throughout the country (SNH, 1998). Nevertheless, this potential has yet to be fully realised, and there is still considerable room for further improvement and a more widespread adoption of the principle of integration.

Internationally, the *Environmental Impact Assessment Directive* has been an important force towards integrating the cultural and natural aspects of landscape within the planning arena in recent years. There are also several new landscape initiatives which could prove important for both the cultural and natural aspects of landscape in the future, if endorsed nationally. Most notable are the Council of Europe's *Recommendation on the Integrated Conservation of Cultural Landscape Areas as Part of Landscape Policies,* and their *European Landscape Convention;* in addition there is the International Union for the Conservation of Nature's *Pan-European Biological and Landscape Diversity Strategy;* while the European Union's *European Spatial Development Perspective* may prove particularly influential. Together these are likely to encourage an approach to landscape which combines its cultural and natural aspects, integrates both of these with planning for development and land management, and links them to sustainable development. These are surely worthwhile aims for the future.

IMPLEMENTATION

In presenting Historic Scotland's vision and associated strategic objectives for the historic landscape, we recognise that many others have a vital role to play in shaping the future of Scotland's historic landscape, both on their own account and in partnership with HS. Consequently, we intend to consult widely on the aims and objectives presented here. Our most notable partners will continue to be Local Authorities, RCAHMS, Scottish Natural Heritage, sister Government Departments, the Forestry Commission, and voluntary sector organisations such as the Council for Scottish Archaeology, the National Trust for Scotland and Scottish Environment Link, together with individual owners and occupiers. In addition, we hope to encourage the involvement of other public agencies, such as the Scottish Environmental Protection Agency and the National Park Authorities; other voluntary bodies, such as the Royal Society for the Protection of Birds and the Scottish Wildlife Trust; local communities; academic researchers; and interested amateurs to a greater extent than before.

CONCLUSION

Historic Scotland hopes that the development of a coherent strategy for the historic landscape will help foster a more widespread appreciation of the time-depth, historic wealth and cultural diversity within the Scottish landscape. Of course, the process of landscape change will always continue. The aim of the strategy presented here is to help ensure that there is a degree of continuity from the past through the present into the future, thereby allowing the threads of history to be visible in the landscape itself. We also hope that discussions about how the landscape should be managed for the future will gradually become more historically aware. While there will continue to be national priorities and statutorily designated areas, for the future we would like to see more emphasis placed on the value of the landscape as a whole, celebrating its cultural diversity, honouring the common-place and, perhaps most significantly, engaging the community more than has been the case in the past. This is not an easy road to take and success will not come overnight, but it should lead us all in the direction of sustaining the historic landscape for the future, not only in the twenty-first century but also beyond.

REFERENCES

Aalen, F. (ed) (1996). *Landscape Study and Management.* Dublin.

AMBS (1983). Ancient Monuments Board for Scotland, *Thirtieth Annual Report 1983.* Edinburgh HMSO.

Ashmore, P. J. (1994). *Archaeology and the Coastal Erosion Zone: Towards a Historic Scotland Policy.* Historic Scotland.

Atkinson, J.A. (1995). *Medieval or Later Rural Settlement (MOLRS) Study: Recommendations towards a policy statement.* Glasgow University Archaeology Research Division, Glasgow.

Barber, J. and Welsh, J.M. (1992). The potential and the reality: the contribution of archaeology to the green debate, in Macinnes, L. and Wickham-Jones, C.R. (eds), 41-51.

Berry, A.Q. and Brown, I.W. (eds) (1995). *Managing Ancient Monuments: An Integrated Approach.* Clwyd County Council, Clwyd.

Breeze, D.J. (1993). Ancient monuments legislation, in Hunter J. and Ralston, I. (eds), 44-55.

Breeze, D.J. (1994). Marketing our past, in Fladmark, J.M. (ed) *Cultural Tourism,* 237-247. Aberdeen.

Brunskill, R.W. (1987). *Traditional Farm Buildings of Britain.* London.

Callander, R. (1998). *How Scotland is owned.* Edinburgh.

Callander, R. and Wightman, A. (eds) (1998). *Understanding Land Reform in Scotland.* University of Edinburgh.

Clark, K. (1993). Sustainable Development and the Historic Environment, in Swain, H. (ed) *Rescuing the Historic Environment,* 87-90. RESCUE, Herts.

Countryside Commission, English Heritage and English Nature (1996). *Ideas into Action for Local Agenda 21: conservation initiatives in the local environment.*

Countryside Commission, English Heritage, English Nature and Environment Agency (1997). *What Matters and Why - Environmental Capital: A New Approach.*

Darvill, T, Gerrard, C and Startin, B. (1993). Identifying and protecting historic landscapes, *Antiquity,* 67, 563-74.

Dennison, E.P. and Coleman, R. (1998). *Historic Melrose: the archaeological implications of development.* The Scottish Burgh Survey, HS in association with Scottish Cultural Press.

Dennison, E.P. and Stones, J. (1997). *Historic Aberdeen: the archaeological implications of development.* The Scottish Burgh Survey, HS in association with Scottish Cultural Press.

DES (1998). *Discovery and Excavation in Scotland.* Council for Scottish Archaeology, Edinburgh.

Dunwell, A.J. and Trout, R.C. (1999). Burrowing Animals and Archaeology. HS *Technical Advice Note 16.*

Dyson Bruce, L, Dixon, P, Hingley and R, Stevenson, J (1999). *Historic Landuse Assessment (HLA): Development and Potential of a Technique for Assessing Historic Landuse Patterns.* HS and RCAHMS, Edinburgh.

English Heritage (1997). *Sustaining the historic environment: new perspectives on the future.* English Heritage Discussion Document, London.

Herring, P. (1998). *Cornwall's Historic Landscape: presenting a method of historic landscape assessment.* Cornwall Archaeological Unit, Cornwall.

Hingley, R. (ed) (1993). *Medieval or Later Rural Settlement in Scotland: Management and Preservation*. HS Occasional Paper No.1, Edinburgh.

Hingley, R, Ashmore, P, Clarke, C. and Sheridan, A. (1999). Peat, archaeology and palaeoecology, in Coles, B, Coles, J and Jørgensen (eds) *Bog Bodies, Sacred Sites and Wetland Archaeology*, 105-114. WARP Occasional Paper 12, Exeter.

Holdsworth, P. (ed) (1987). *Excavations in the Medieval Burgh of Perth 1979–81*. Society of Antiquaries of Scotland Monograph Series No. 5, Edinburgh.

HS (1994). *Historic Scotland Framework Document*. Historic Scotland, October 1994.

HS (1998a). *Memorandum of Guidance on listed buildings and conservation areas*. Edinburgh.

HS (1998b). Medieval or Later Rural Settlement: Historic Scotland's Approach. *HS Archaeology* Paper no.7, Edinburgh

HS and SNH (1995). *A Statement of Intent Between Historic Scotland and Scottish Natural Heritage*. HS and SNH, Edinburgh.

Hunter, J. and Ralston, I. (eds) (1993). *Archaeological Resource Management in the UK: An Introduction*. Stroud.

Iles, R. (1992). Integrated conservation management on private estates, in Macinnes, L. and Wickham-Jones, C.R. (eds), 134-9.

Jacques, D. (1995). The Rise of Cultural Landscapes, *International Journal of Heritage Studies 1* (2), 91-101.

Lambrick, G. (1992). The importance of the cultural heritage in a green world: towards the development of landscape integrity assessment, in Macinnes, L. and Wickham-Jones, C.R. (eds), 105-126.

Macinnes, L. (1993a). Archaeology as land use, in Hunter, J. and Ralston, R. (eds), 243-55.

Macinnes, L. (1993b). Towards a common language: the unifying perceptions of an integrated approach, in Fladmark J.M. (ed) *Heritage: Conservation, Interpretation and Enterprise,* 101-111. Aberdeen.

Macinnes, L. and Wickham-Jones, C.R. (1992). Time-depth in the countryside: archaeology and the environment, in Macinnes, L. and Wickham-Jones, C.R. (eds), 1-13.

Macinnes, L. and Wickham-Jones, C.R. (eds) (1992). *All Natural Things: Archaeology and the Green Debate*. Oxbow Monograph 21, Oxford.

Mackay, D. (1993). Scottish rural Highland settlement: preserving a people's past, in Hingley, R. (ed), 43-51.

McNeely, J.A. and Keeton, W.S. (1995). The Interaction between Biological and Cultural Diversity, in Von Droste, B., Plachter, H. and Rossler, M. (eds), 24-37.

Miles, J. (1992). Environmental conservation and archaeology: is there a need for integrated designations? in Macinnes, L. and Wickham-Jones, C.R. (eds), 97-104.

Muir, R. (1999). *Approaches to landscape*. London.

Murray, J.C. (1983). The Scottish Burgh Survey – a review, *Proc Soc Antiq Scot* 113, 1-10.

Naismith, R.J. (1985). *Buildings of the Scottish Countryside*. London.

NPPG 5 (1994). National Planning Policy Guideline, Archaeology and Planning. The Scottish Office, Edinburgh.

NPPG 18 (1999). *National Planning Policy Guideline, Planning and the Historic*

Environment. The Scottish Office, Edinburgh.

Owen, O. (forthcoming). Protecting the Archaeology of Scotland's Historic Towns, in Dennison, E.P. (ed) *Conservation and Change in Historic Towns*. Council for British Archaeology, *Research Report* 122, 47–59.

Prott, L. (1992). A common heritage: the World Heritage Convention, in Macinnes, L. and Wickham-Jones, C.R. (eds), 65–86.

RCAHMS (1990). *North-East Perth: an archaeological landscape*. Royal Commission on the Ancient and Historical Monuments of Scotland, Edinburgh.

RCAHMS (1994). *South-East Perth: an archaeological landscape*. Royal Commission on the Ancient and Historical Monuments of Scotland, Edinburgh.

RCAHMS (1997). *Eastern Dumfriesshire: an archaeological landscape*. Royal Commission on the Ancient and Historical Monuments of Scotland, Edinburgh.

RCAHMS (1998). *Forts, Farms and Furnaces: Archaeology in the Central Scotland Forest*. Royal Commission on the Ancient and Historical Monuments of Scotland, Edinburgh.

Rossler, M. (1995). UNESCO and Cultural Landscape Protection, in Von Droste, B., Plachter, H. and Rossler, M. (eds), 42–9.

SNH (1997). *Provoke, Relate, Reveal: SNH's Policy Framework for Interpretation*. Scottish Natural Heritage, Perth.

SNH (1998). *National Parks for Scotland, SNH's Advice to Government*. Scottish Natural Heritage, Perth.

SNH (1999). *National Scenic Areas: A Consultation paper*. Scottish Natural Heritage, Perth.

Tilden, F. (1957). *Interpreting our heritage*. North Carolina.

Von Droste, B., Plachter, H. and Rossler, M. (eds) (1995). *Cultural Landscapes of Universal Value*. UNESCO.

ACKNOWLEDGEMENTS

This paper benefited greatly from the discussion at the conference in Battleby where it was originally presented, and from the comments of several colleagues within Historic Scotland. Particular thanks must go to Professors David Breeze and Bill Hanson for their helpful comments on earlier drafts of the text.

3

Pressure Points: Farmers, Foresters and Archaeologists

JEAN BALFOUR

INTRODUCTION

This perspective comes from one who is a landowner and manager, a farmer and a forester, but who has also a passionate involvement in the natural world of Scotland in general and its northern parts in particular.

The second half of the twentieth century has seen significant investment in primary production from the land. Support by successive governments (and the EU) for agriculture and investment in both the growing and utilisation of trees have created industries, which have been generally prosperous. Today, however, land managers are faced with a rather different situation since returns for all primary products have declined sharply, confidence levels are low and there is apprehension for the future. Agriculture, and particularly forestry, are long term and depend on stability as well as economic viability to flourish. A well-managed countryside depends on their prosperity.

AWARENESS AND PUBLIC INTEREST

Another change, which has taken place over the years, is the increased public interest in how the land is used. Conservation and recreation are seen as an integral part of land management and the right of public opinion is recognised. However these interests also depend on a well-managed countryside and the prosperity to achieve this.

Environmental awareness and greater public interest in how and sometimes where different types of land-use are put into practice have increased. In agriculture this has been re-enforced by EU schemes and regulation particularly for stock (animal) movements and traceability requirements following BSE. These arrangements make further demands on land managers.

Forestry, however, remains the most regulated rural land-use. Agreement by the Forestry Authority to plant trees on previously unforested land requires a quite complicated procedure. Applicants have to supply full details of their proposals for new planting and thinning as well as for the felling of existing woods. This has to be agreed with Forestry Authority and notified to Historic Scotland or the Local Authority Archaeologist for comment. The application is put on the public register, providing an opportunity for all and sundry to comment. This takes four weeks. Thereafter it is sent to the statutory consultees, usually the Planning Authority and Scottish Natural Heritage (SNH). Failure to reach agreement to the proposals can result in the application being referred to the Regional Advisory Committee (RAC) and even ultimately the Secretary of State. The final decision is issued by the Forestry Commission. Of course, if the proposed area needs an Environmental Assessment, the time is even longer. It can be argued that land-use change can impact on both landscape and nature conservation and that such change must be carefully monitored. However, there is always a balance to be found between the public's right to intervene and sensible land-use activity. Those who comment need to recognise that they, too, have a responsibility to provide informed and objective comments.

CONSULTATION AND NATURE CONSERVATION

Forestry (and agriculture in general) are not subject to the planning acts. The special arrangements which control forestry have developed for the private sector since 1975. Why, then, were agriculture and forestry and their related buildings exempted from planning control? Post-war, the planning acts were in their infancy and were directed at town rehabilitation, housing and urban development. How to make sure that concrete in one form or another did not impinge on good agricultural land or on sites of nature conservation interest was the main objective. The countryside had to be protected from such development. Primary production at that time was seen as countryside activity and as such part of the landscape and pattern of the land. At the same time identification of special nature conservation sites began – SSSIs were seen mainly as protection from urban development. Special consultation arrangements for SSSIs were therefore incorporated into planning procedures. This often meant that identification and designation of SSSIs was less in more remote rural areas where development was seen as an unlikely threat. Caithness and Sutherland were examples of this.

LAND-USE CHANGE IN THE COUNTRYSIDE – THE ROLE OF THE SSSIS AND NSAS

The shift of interest towards land-use change within the countryside as an emerging issue took place in the seventies. At that time, the Nature Conservancy Council (NCC) provided a paper on Agriculture and Conservation targeting, in particular, intensive arable farming, mainly in England, but not exclusively so. The importance of stock and mixed farming in Scotland provided 'safeguards' for nature conservation which the paper did not always fully recognise. The NCC also attempted a paper on Forestry and Nature Conservation which, after several false starts, appeared in the early eighties and coincided with the ill-advised planting programmes in East Sutherland and Caithness.

Prime nature conservation sites in the countryside took on a new significance. Thanks to the vision of the Nature Conservancy, the Nature Conservation Review (NCR) provided the basis for the identification and designation of prime sites on which the SSSI system was developed.

The whole process recognised that there had to be a hierarchical approach, which identified the best sites taking account of local circumstances and rarity. This approach has been crucial not only in the conservation of important sites but also in raising awareness. It included a recognition of nature conservation values and their legitimate place in decision making in land-use change, and an awareness that although everything cannot be safeguarded, at least a good sample of what is valuable should be conserved. This has been followed by non-statutory (advisory) lists such as the Scottish Wildlife Trust's 'listed wildlife sites' and also better understanding of nature conservation values in land management.

Attitudes towards SSSIs have not always been positive. The legislation of 1981 which brought in the concept of damaging operations was often looked on as unreasonable by those who felt they were already managing their land well. Nevertheless, at that time a need was seen to underpin SSSIs more firmly and to provide greater protection. Had the act been better constructed and at times better implemented, problems would have been less.

Nature conservation provides a useful example of how their special sites came to be identified and designated as SSSIs, and made a part of the planning and forestry regulatory measures. By their very nature they predominated in the countryside but are certainly not absent in urban fringe areas. Archaeological sites are perhaps more widespread and can be found in both rural and urban situations. They, too, are the subjects of a designation process called 'scheduling'. This process is based on criteria laid down by the Ancient Monuments Board for Scotland and carried out by Historic Scotland. SSSIs didn't just emerge, however; they are and have been based on increasingly rigorous procedures, which followed from the NCR and the science on which it was based. Criteria were further refined and can be used throughout Great Britain. Though not initially comprehensive, the system provided a fundamental base and criteria.

Criticism of SSSIs still remain, with accusations of sterilisation of large areas (twelve per cent of the land area of Scotland). However, had the important nature conservation areas of East Sutherland and Caithness been within the SSSI system instead of being omitted, the saga of the Flow Country might never have happened.

Today, SSSIs have their place within the consultation mechanism of the planning acts and the consultations that take place over woodland grant schemes. In agriculture, they impinge on grant schemes and provide a background at least to Environmentally Sensitive Areas and Countryside Premium Schemes. Perhaps their 'influence' is greatest in Woodland Grant Schemes. New motorways or housing developments can always use the argument, not always reasonably, of overriding public or national interest. What is important here is the way nature conservation and landscape have found a place in recognised procedures and in decision-making on land-use change.

Nature conservation, it can be argued, is not a measure of landscape quality but it is often a significant part of it. The high mountain areas for example, which are a significant part of Scottish landscape, are the home of interesting sub-arctic flora and fauna. It is, therefore, a valuable element within landscape quality and less difficult to quantify. The identification and designation of Natural Scenic Areas (NSA) recognised this in evaluation surveys. They, too, have a place in planning and consultation procedures.

The place of conservation in land-use change and development is not always easy. Prime landscape, for example, though sometimes obvious to the beholder, is inevitably more subjective. Everyone knows that the Queen's View at Loch Tummel, Loch Lomond or the Cuillins are exceptional landscapes even by Scottish standards. However, it has not been possible to effectively reduce this to identifiable elements as in SSSIs. NSAs, which cover thirteen per cent of Scotland and include some SSSIs, are based at least on a systematic approach and have provided an important framework focus on the 'best'. It can well be argued now that thirteen per cent was rather a modest target in a country as beautiful as Scotland, and that there should be an increase. However, previous experience suggests that efforts to identify detailed 'landscape elements' can be both complicated and unsatisfactory as a method.

THE PLACE OF ARCHAEOLOGY

I have spent time on the arrangements for nature conservation and their links with landscape and how these have evolved, because I believe there are lessons to be learnt, which are relevant to archaeology. Legally, the Ancient Monuments and Archaeological Areas Act of 1979 requires the Secretary of State to compile and maintain a schedule of monuments which are of national importance. Of course, archaeologists have long considered archaeological sites of key importance but it is probably fair to say that archaeology has had, at least until recently, less impact either generally or within the decision-making system than nature conservation. It is not correct to say that archaeological sites are necessarily less noticeable than the natural ones, though those below ground certainly are. The Ring of Brodgar, the brochs of the north and west, and Hadrian's Wall are all well known and can be appreciated by those without specialist knowledge. It is a different story when it comes to rig and furrow or apparently obscure flat places or stone heaps. How, one might ask, do they compare in impact on the uninformed with contemplation by those who are not plant biologists of Claish Moss or other important bog sites dominated by unspectacular plants? At least Claish Moss is an SSSI so that observers can understand its place within an important hierarchy. It could, however, be argued that people generally are more interested to learn about artefacts than to understand the dynamics of bog systems. There is a fascination for many in understanding how people lived and worked in conditions so very different from our own. Hoards of jewellery, pottery and even stone axes create a greater rapport and interest for many people than changing vegetation patterns and the call of the dunlin. Yet the many voluntary bodies and groups concerned with nature conservation are stronger and more influential than those concerned with archaeology.

A closer look at SSSIs and scheduled archaeological sites demonstrate some clear differences between the two. SSSIs (1,442 sites in Scotland) are considerably fewer in number than the 6,800 scheduled archaeological sites. On the other hand, the area which is covered by SSSIs is much greater (91,7071 ha). It can be argued, therefore, that SSSIs have a much more significant impact on landscape and land-use change. Perhaps more important is the very large number of unscheduled archaeological sites, which may run to thousands, even tens of thousands. This means that unscheduled sites where knowledge is limited form a significant proportion of all sites, particularly those which are notified to either the Planning Authority or to the Forestry Authority.

Reference has been made to SSSIs and to NSAs and the links between the two. How important is archaeology in the landscape? Perhaps not very important, though some will argue that man's past activity anywhere is archaeological and provides a backdrop for the buildings or artefacts we see. Certain structures such as Ardvreck Castle on Loch Assynt contribute to variety in the near landscape and provide an attractive visual feature. Similarly, the Broch of Mousa, though apparently quite small from the Shetland mainland, provides an impressive edifice when seen from closer range. Many archaeological sites, however, are barely visible, or require special light conditions for previous cultivation to be seen; indeed, many may be underground. The great standing stones of Callanais are compromised by encroaching building rather than rural land-use change. Past land-use must always leave its mark but generally speaking it can be argued that nature conservation is more important than archaeology for landscape conservation.

Because of different acts and procedures there are differences between the way in which the conservation of nature and landscape are handled on the one hand and archaeology on the other. Since the merger between the Countryside Commission for Scotland and the Nature Conservancy Council, one organisation, Scottish Natural Heritage, is now responsible for nature conservation and landscape. Some local authorities have their own archaeologist and some do not. In the latter case, the responsibility then falls to Historic Scotland and their area inspectors. As a land manager, therefore, it is easy to feel part of an uneasy triangle and not to be sure who has the last word.

Let us look then at how archaeology impinges on the land manager in the course of his or her work. Where there is relatively little change in activity, say on farmland, which has long been under cultivation, things can continue much as they are. Standing stones, for example, continue untouched even if awkwardly situated in the middle of fields. It is where land-use change is contemplated that issues arise: for example, the ploughing out of permanent pasture in the sixties for increased cereal acreage.

As mentioned earlier in this paper, forestry, particularly new planting, creates significant land-use change, which is probably why it has become the most highly regulated countryside activity. It is not intended to discuss here whether or not this should be modified. I want to look at archaeology's place in these arrangements and consider some of the problems which relate to it in principle and practice, and to try to address some of the difficulties which arise from insufficient knowledge of the archaeological resource and the apparent lack of a comprehensive framework. Applicants usually start with some knowledge of conservation value: for example, whether an area includes an SSSI or is in a NSA. Of course, they may need a more detailed appraisal, but at least an SSSI and a NSA are benchmarks. As already remarked, the scheduling of archaeological sites is far from comprehensive and a high percentage of sites notified to the Forestry Authority are therefore unscheduled.

CONSULTATION

When even a comparatively modest new planting scheme lands on the Forest Authority's desk, an archaeological survey may be required and has then to be commissioned. Such a survey, is quite rightly, funded by Historic Scotland because many important sites are still to be scheduled. However, this is likely to cause delay and frustration. Land managers expect that the necessary information should be to hand 'if it is an important site' and that there should be some hierarchical approach. In these circumstances, areas unidentifiable to the archaeologically ignorant can be put forward as significant. Even nineteenth-century cultivation such as rig and furrow can be considered important though difficult for the unpractised eye to see. Of course, there should be recognition of artefacts and past activities of interest on a given site, but they are probably not understood by the land manager and cannot, as is the case with SSSI or NSA, be clearly related to a national framework.

Because archaeological sites are much more numerous than the key sites of the natural world, it can be argued that there are inevitably numerous unscheduled sites still to be described. It could also be argued that this is not limited to archaeology, the natural world has, even in Scotland, many unknowns, particularly among arthropod invertebrates or even lichen communities, and their conservation remains fragmentary. Nevertheless, further SSSI designations are not numerous and do not detract from an accepted national framework. National Scenic Areas are also well understood. Any increase in the latter would be the subject of a consultation exercise with other interests.

Archaeology, as was touched on earlier, does not have the same public awareness levels as nature and landscape conservation and this is not helpful. Nature conservation has been fortunate in that the time was right: the David Attenborough programmes in the seventies led to a tremendous step forward in awareness. Perhaps if Magnus Magnusson had done a series of archaeological programmes called 'Our Past Inheritance' instead of 'Mastermind', archaeological awareness could have grown on a similar scale.

It has been suggested that links between Scottish Natural Heritage and Historic Scotland could be strengthened or that something more formal could be created – a merger? Personally, I do not believe this would be helpful, either generally or from the land manager's point of view. The bodies are different and a wider range of functions for one organisation would not be practical. Indeed, SNH still has to get up to speed on its own range of interests. Perhaps it would have helped awareness, however, if Historic Scotland had become a quango like English Heritage.

A WAY FORWARD

It is difficult for a mere land manager to suggest how to tackle these problems but the following points could be considered.

1. Tackling the problem of unscheduled sites. This might include clearer priorities for different types of sites and more preliminary surveys.

2. Addressing in practical terms the issue of how much of any particular type of site should be scheduled. Priorities and choices will always be necessary.

3. The relationship between national and local interest in scheduling.

4. Streamlining the links and arrangements between local authority planning and local authority archaeologists.

5. Streamlining the relationship between local authority archaeologists and Historic Scotland, including the development of local plans and priorities.

6. Making the relationships and consultation between Historic Scotland and land managers more user-friendly.

Perhaps key to all are better relationships and better understanding of archaeology by land managers. Promoting this lies primarily in the hands of archaeologists. As land managers we accept the place of responsible public interest in land-use change. We need economic stability to deliver.

4

Forest Enterprise in Wales: Heritage and Environmental Data Capture

CAROLINE EARWOOD

INTRODUCTION

Forestry Commission woodlands in Wales are primarily new forests planted during the 1940s, '50s and '60s, covering an area in excess of 125,000 hectares. The forests cover a variety of terrains, from the upland plateaux of Denbighshire in North Wales to the steep valleys of South Wales. The archaeology of these areas is similarly varied, with remains of former agricultural and industrial landscapes spanning the early prehistoric to the modern period.

Forest Enterprise is committed to managing its estate in a manner which will sustain the environmental and productive potential of the forests whilst at the same time produce the financial, social and other outputs required by Ministers and the Forestry Commissioners. One of Forest Enterprise's objectives is to manage its forests in harmony with the character and heritage of the countryside.

Forest Enterprise (Wales) is run by five Forest Districts who are responsible for the implementation of agreed plans in the most cost effective and efficient manner. The Districts report to the Regional Director who is located in Aberystwyth.

Responsibility for the protection of archaeology in Wales rests primarily with Cadw (Welsh Historic Monuments) and the four Welsh Archaeological Trusts who maintain the sites and monuments records and provide archaeological management advice.

THE WELSH HERITAGE ASSETS PROJECT

During the last decade it has become increasingly apparent that knowledge of archaeology within the Welsh forests was extremely poor. The sites and monuments records, established during the 1970s, had recorded few sites on Forestry Commission land. This is a legacy of the creation of the forests prior to the creation of the sites and monuments records and at a time when there was little systematic archaeological survey. The lack of good archaeological data presents serious problems to Forest Enterprise in the management of its landholding and the protection of the heritage of Wales.

Until 1995, proposals to remedy this situation had foundered on the high cost of survey based on traditional archaeological methods and the lack of a coherent strategy for incorporating archaeological data into a management system. However, with the increasing use of Geographical Information Systems (GIS) and a wider understanding of Forest Enterprise working practices, both difficulties have been overcome.

In 1996/97, Forest Enterprise (Wales) commissioned the Clwyd-Powys Archaeological Trust to carry out a pilot survey covering *c*.14,000 hectares in a number of locations throughout Wales. The pilot survey established the methodology of the project, provided baseline costings and was an important factor in Forest Enterprise (Wales) obtaining funding from the Heritage Lottery Fund to extend the survey to the rest of the Welsh estate. In planning the Welsh Heritage Assets Project, Forest Enterprise took account of work both within the Forestry Commission and in other organisations, most notably survey work on the North York Moors (Lee, 1995), management systems developed by the Forestry Commission in the New Forest, and the First Edition Project of the Royal Commission on the Ancient and Historical Monuments of Scotland. Management guidelines take account of the Forestry Commission *Forests and Archaeology Guidelines* and *Forestry and Archaeology in Scotland* (Barclay, 1992).

The Welsh Heritage Assets project commenced in November 1998 and aimed to be completed within three years. To date, over 30,000 hectares of land have been surveyed and contracts have recently been awarded for survey of a further 45,000 hectares.

The objectives of the Welsh Heritage Assets Project are:

1.   To identify and map sites and areas of archaeological interest.
2.   To record their nature, condition, landscape context and date.
3.   To place the sites in different categories of importance.
4.   To advise on the management of archaeological sites.
5.   To make recommendations for further recording/investigations.
6.   To advise on the presentation of archaeological sites and data to the public.

ARCHAEOLOGICAL SURVEY METHODOLOGY

The archaeological survey commences with the digitisation of features from the second edition Ordnance Survey 6-inch series maps which are rectified to modern Ordnance Survey National Grid. The data is stored as MapInfo tables, depicting and describing natural features, such as bogs, ponds, water courses, former woodland and significant rock outcrops; man-made features, such as structures, trackways and physical boundaries, such as walls and hedgerows; and political features, such as parish boundaries.

The survey contractor is obliged to consult the regional sites and monuments record, air photographs, later editions of the Ordnance Survey maps where significant changes have taken place in the landscape, and Forest Enterprise records such as forest design plans and coupe management plans. In addition, it may be appropriate to consult tithe maps, Ordnance Survey surveyors' drawings, first edition Ordnance Survey and tithe maps, estate maps and records, the National Monuments Record and the records of Cadw, the unitiary authorities and the national parks.

Desk-based analysis of these records results in the creation of point data, locating archaeological sites. The GIS tables are then depicted against the digitised outlines of the Forest Enterprise sub-compartments, thus making it possible to reconcile the former and present landscape. This is a key tool in aiding the location of sites on the ground. At this stage the results of the desk-based study are verified in the field. During site visiting, the project officer is normally accompanied by a Forest Enterprise employee, who provides local knowledge of the road system, forest structure and often information about the pre-forest landscape which is rarely recorded on paper. The aim of site visiting is to check on the location and condition of sites, and to provide recommendations for their management and potential for scheduling and public access improvements. All sites visited will be categorised as being of national (A), regional or local importance (B), of lesser significance (C), or having no physical presence. The project is achieving a visiting rate of between 60 to 75 per cent of all sites. Those sites which are not visited, categorised as Not Yet Evaluated, are usually inaccessible at the time of survey. A system for reporting sites has been developed within Forest Enterprise (Wales) so that the remaining sites can be located and evaluated prior to harvesting.

Following site visiting, the point data table will be edited and area data depicting archaeologically sensitive areas, scheduled ancient monuments and archaeological landscapes will be created. It is now understood by Forest Enterprise employees in Wales that archaeological sites cannot be adequately depicted by spots on maps and that advice in the *Forests and Archaeology Guidelines*, to restrict planting to within 20 metres of an archaeological site, is difficult to apply if the extent of the site is not clearly depicted. Therefore large and more complex sites, such as clusters of buildings, are depicted as sensitive areas. The depiction of the pre-forestry landscape within the GIS allows forest officers to plan forest operations with due regard not only to the sites represented by point and area data but linear sites such as stone walls, hedgerows, banks and trackways. The constraints of modern forestry do not allow the preservation of all such features in their entirety but forward planning of forest operations minimises damage. Where site visiting identifies particularly well-preserved and significant elements of the pre-forestry landscape, these are depicted as archaeological landscapes to raise awareness of their importance.

INTEGRATION OF THE SURVEY DATA INTO FOREST ENTERPRISE MANAGEMENT SYSTEMS

Forest Officers are today required to manage a wide range of environmental and heritage issues, whilst at the same time producing timber in a highly competitive market. It is essential that any form of environmental and heritage data is packaged in a user-friendly format which facilitates ease of access and good management. It is equally important that Forest Enterprise staff receive training in archaeological site recognition and management. This is achieved by archaeological training seminars in which a range of sites of different types and periods are examined, and management options discussed.

Following testing for compliance with the *Brief for Archaeological Survey*, the data is converted into ArcView, the Forest Enterprise system, and presented through a customised 'front-end' constructed by the GeoData Institute, University of Southampton. This allows interrogation of the data through primary record number (PRN), site type, scheduled ancient monument (SAM), compartment and name. Forest officers are expected to understand the data they are handling but they are not expected to be archaeologists. Therefore a series of glossaries have been embedded in the query functions, providing information on site type, period and site categories. In addition to providing a short description, the site type glossary gives examples of common locations, common management problems and management recommendations for each site type. Where a site type is complex or large, with implications for the forest structure, design suggestions that may protect and enhance the environment of the site are made.

Customised spatial queries have also been designed to allow officers to determine quickly what archaeological features may be affected by forest operations, such as harvesting or thinning, within any given coupe. Whilst every effort has been made to ensure accuracy of location of the archaeological and forest stock data, it is not surprising in the conversion of data from old maps to GIS that perfect accuracy is unobtainable. Therefore, spatial queries permit a variable buffer zone to be set. Forest operations may create new areas of disturbance, which do not conform to compartment or coupe boundaries. These may be queried by the creation of temporary areas or lines representing proposed roads, car parks, quarries, etc. Such spatial queries will search for point, line and area data which is within or which intersects with the proposed area of activity.

The primary purpose of the customised GIS is the protection of archaeological sites and landscapes within the day-to-day management of the forest. However, in achieving the objective of improving public access to sites and data, the GIS may be used by recreation rangers and officers drawing up plans for enhanced public presentation or events in the forest. For a variety of reasons it is considered desirable that as many sites as possible should be illustrated with scanned images taken from the photographic record made as part of each survey contract. The image can be displayed in conjunction with details of the site location, description, condition, management recommendations, i.e., the fields from the SMR table which constitutes the point data.

The first version of the customised GIS went on trial in one District in Wales in the winter of 1998/99. During 1999 the remaining four Districts received data in GIS format together with any modifications to the structure of the GIS required in the light of the trial.

In order to ensure the proper management of nationally important sites (category A) it is a requirement that the Districts prepare management plans for all such sites, whether or not they are scheduled ancient monuments. Management plans are prepared using the *Archaeological Database* consisting of the SMR table, which Forest officers are not permitted to edit, linked to an Objective table and a Prescriptions table. The Prescriptions table allows forest officers to list remedial action required to improve and maintain the environment of the site with details of personnel, dates of work and costings. A number of standard reports allow this data to be displayed and printed in a variety of ways, including as a site management plan, which, if the site is scheduled, will be submitted to Cadw for approval as a SAM plan. The *Archaeological Database*, which was created by a forest officer, is linked to the Operational Planning Module (OPM) which is used in Wales to link various aspects of forest planning into one coherent system.

THE ROLE OF THE ARCHAEOLOGICAL TRUSTS

All archaeological data from the survey on Forestry Commission land in Wales is passed in digital form to the four SMRs in Wales who are now maintaining a record in MapInfo format. This data forms part of the SMRs and is therefore in the public domain. In order to ensure that the data is regularly updated as new information becomes available, Forest Enterprise have agreed a data exchange procedure with the SMRs.

Each Forest District has a nominated Archaeological Liaison Officer, who is part of the forest planning team. This officer is able to record new information within the 'local records' of the *Archaeological Database*. Such information may be collected by tarriffing teams, rangers or forest officers during their normal working day. At regular intervals, presently six months, the new data is passed, in digital form, to the archaeological Trusts who integrate it into the SMRs and return an updated file, including any new data recorded by themselves since the last data exchange.

During forest operations, new or previously unvisited sites may be located. In many cases forest officers are competent to determine the correct methods of site management. However, it is essential that such sites are visited by an archaeologist who will more fully assess their character, age, condition and correct category. During the life of the Welsh Heritage Assets Project, sites may be visited by the Archaeological Co-ordinator, but the normal practice is that the Districts will seek advice from the relevant archaeological Trust. To ensure that this process runs smoothly, the Districts have recently signed site-visiting agreements with the Trusts. Additionally, Forest Enterprise provides the Trusts with an annual outline of harvesting plans and makes available for inspection the Forest Design Plans and the schedule of plan revisions. Forest Enterprise (Wales) regional office provides a summary of these arrangements for the Districts in *The Archaeological Management Guidelines*.

ENVIRONMENTAL DATA

The archaeological survey has highlighted the strong links between the historic and natural environment. In many cases archaeological sites are within Sites of Wildlife Conservation Value designated by Forest Enterprise, Sites of Special Scientific Interest (SSSIs) or sites identified by the local Wildlife Trusts. More commonly, however, archaeological sites are unrecorded pockets of biodiversity within the conifer crop. Spoil heaps of former copper and lead mines may be host to rare species of lichens and bryophytes, old buildings may support a variety of ferns, former farmsteads may be associated with broad-leaf trees, such as sycamore and ash, which provide nesting sites for birds of prey, and ice-houses or mine levels may be home to bats.

In order to ensure that environmental sites can be managed as competently as the archaeological sites, it is essential that the paper records maintained by Forest Enterprise are converted into GIS format and management systems developed which allow management plans to be written within this framework. An audit of existing records will also highlight deficiencies of knowledge, which can be addressed by future survey work.

A pilot project is currently being undertaken to establish the best methodology of converting this data into a GIS format with direct links to the archaeological tables and query routines. An assessment is also being made of how this data can be formatted to ensure compatibility with the records of other bodies and eventually be linked to the National Biodiversity Network.

REFERENCES

Barclay, G.J. (1992). Forestry and Archaeology in Scotland. *Scottish Forestry* 46(1), 27-47.

Forestry Commission (1995). *Forests and Archaeology Guidelines*. Edinburgh.

Lee, G. (1995). Forestry Management and Archaeology. In *Managing Ancient Monuments: An Integrated Approach*, Berry, A.Q. and Brown, I. W (eds), Clwyd Archaeology Service, 97-104.

5

Recent Developments in Recording Scotland's Historic Landscapes

J. B. Stevenson and L. Dyson Bruce

Introduction

This paper discusses some of the recent developments in archaeological survey and, in particular, considers three projects, two of which have been jointly funded by the Royal Commission on the Ancient and Historical Monuments of Scotland and Historic Scotland. The three projects, the Historic Land-use Assessment Project (HLA), the First Edition Survey Project (FESP), and the Central Scotland Forest Survey reflect many of the changes in the nature of archaeological recording that have taken place in the last two decades. Whilst all three projects are broad in their scope and are concerned with archaeology in a landscape setting, they address very different archaeological and historical problems. FESP is closely focused on a specific range of monuments on a nation-wide basis, the Central Scotland Forest Survey concentrates on a relatively small geographical area but covers monuments of all periods, while HLA assesses the landscape of Scotland as a whole. Nevertheless, all three projects were designed to illuminate and record the development of the Scottish landscape in ways that have not hitherto been attempted.

Underpinning all three projects is the Royal Commission's GIS system which, although only introduced into the National Monuments Record of Scotland (NMRS) a few years ago, is now a fundamental tool for handling archaeological data. Without GIS it would be impractical to manipulate or interrogate the data in the ways that will be described, and, in the longer term, the success of these projects will be measured by the use that is made of the large amount of information contained within the GIS system.

Over the last two decades, the range of material that is considered to be of archaeological interest has broadened and deepened. Broadened in the sense that we have moved on from studying individual monuments to analysing monuments in a landscape setting and, secondly, to seeing the modern landscape itself as an archaeological monument, albeit comprising elements dating from prehistoric times to the present day. These developments have helped to reinforce the view commonly held by archaeologists that archaeology is not a closely-defined discipline but comprises a series of techniques for analysing the past and, as the subject has deepened and broadened, so the range of analytical techniques has also widened.

Traditionally, there have been strong links between archaeologists and historians, but it is noteworthy that Scotland, with certain distinguished exceptions, has not benefited from the development of historical geography comparable with that seen in England. The recent advances in what is loosely referred to as landscape archaeology have, to a certain extent, taken us beyond the scope of historical geography into a much broader field of research that embraces not only the study of the physical remains of the cultural landscape but also the interplay between the natural and man-made environment.

HISTORIC LAND-USE ASSESSMENT

The Historic Land-use Assessment Project was established by Historic Scotland and the Royal Commission to explore the viability of creating a method of assessing historic land-use patterns in Scotland. Its origins lie in Landscape Character Assessment (SNH, 1998), which has generated a new and more informed approach to landscape issues. This particular project was precipitated by the landscape character assessment programme initiated by Scottish Natural Heritage, and HS and RCAHMS would like to acknowledge the help and support received from SNH staff during the course of the project.

The scale of resolution used in most landscape character assessments does not enable the historical and archaeological dimensions of landscape development to be integrated into the mapping process, but they are fundamental to our understanding of the landscape as it is today. In order to address this problem, a number of Historic Land-use Character Assessment studies were undertaken in Britain, and the present project has drawn heavily on the work undertaken in Cornwall, where in the early 1990s a pioneering attempt was made to map the county's historic field patterns (Herring, 1998). The present Historic Land-use Assessment Project was established in 1996 and was charged with designing a methodology for mapping archaeological and historic land-use patterns that could be applied throughout Scotland.

Unlike earlier attempts which were based on paper maps, the HLA programme uses the Royal Commission GIS system and, as a result, it is able to integrate the information with other datasets already contained within the system.

The mapping process involves the systematic assessment of topographic OS maps, archaeological and historical data, the Macaulay Institute's Landcover of Scotland 1988 Survey, and vertical aerial photographs taken from 1947 to the present day. The information from the various sources is collated and mapped by the application of a simple, but clearly defined, series of historical land-use types. The data is captured at a scale of 1:25,000 and mapped on to an overlay. The resulting composite map is then entered into the GIS system to produce topologically correct maps. Once entered into the GIS, the completed maps are transferred into Artemis, a more user-friendly Windows-based system. The maps can then be combined with other datasets for further interrogation and analysis.

The land-use types that have been defined reflect readily identifiable historical entities. For ease of use, two main categories of land-use type have been defined:

1. Current Landuse Types

Reflecting historic land-use types in current use, which may include types that are in origin several hundred years old, and

2. Relict Landuse Types

Reflecting historic land-use types that have been abandoned, but which still leave some trace in the landscape.

Any feature which is less than one hectare in extent is deemed to be too small to plot. In practice, this means that many archaeological sites do not appear on the initial HLA maps, but they can, of course, be shown by introducing the National Monuments Record of Scotland point-data layer on the GIS.

While establishing the methodology, a variety of landscapes were studied, ranging from Skye, where the relationships between crofting, pre-Improvement settlement and the impact of recent forestry were addressed; to north-east Fife, where prehistoric cropmark landscapes, designed landscapes and field-pattern changes since the last war were of particular interest; and to the relict industrial landscapes associated with the coal, iron and lime industries of western Fife.

Having established the methodology in the first year, a further range of areas was mapped, including part of the eastern Cairngorms, the eastern end of the Antonine Wall, part of Mainland Orkney and Sanday, and a section of

Liddesdale centred on Newcastleton. In 1998, as part of the preparation for Scottish national parks, attention was focused on Loch Lomond and the Trossachs, and work is proceeding on the remainder of the possible Cairngorms park area. In addition to the work funded by Historic Scotland, the project has been expanded to take in partnership ventures, such as work undertaken on behalf of SNH on Rum and the Forestry Commission in eastern Dumfriesshire.

Much of the analysis for the project is based on the interpretation of vertical aerial photographs, such as the view of Newcastleton in Liddesdale shown in Plate 1, and it is fortunate that the Royal Commission houses the national collection of vertical and oblique aerial photographs. The photograph shows grid pattern of the eighteenth-century planned village, surrounded by a network of small fields, which, in fact, are crofts associated with the village houses. Around them are the post-improvement rectilinear fields, while beyond the fields there is what appears to be open moorland. The HLA map of the current land-use of the valley (Plate 2) shows the lower ground picked out in the buff of rectilinear improvement fields of the late eighteenth and nineteenth centuries. The large commercial forestry plantations stand out in green on the east side, which contrasts with the olive of the surviving improved pasture and the purple of the managed grouse-moors on the west side. Contained within this pattern of modern land-use there are areas of relict prehistoric and medieval landscapes, shown cross-hatched. The village of Newcastleton appears in magenta and is surrounded on the south by the pink of the crofts, now largely a relict landscape, as they are no longer all worked on an individual basis by the villagers. The bright green towards the top of the map is also of historical interest as it is an area of designed landscape around one of the improvement period farms.

Using the GIS, the data can be interrogated and, on Plate 3, areas of relict archaeological and historic landscapes have been selected. They are shown here representing three separate chronological periods – prehistoric (in brown); medieval (in deep pink); and post-medieval (in pale pink). The prehistoric blocks are areas of Iron Age settlements and farms, the medieval landscapes are largely blocks of farmland carved out of the medieval royal hunting forest, and the post-medieval landscape comprises blocks of fields laid out in the seventeenth and eighteenth centuries, which were not subsequently incorporated into the late-eighteenth- and nineteenth-century grid pattern of fields.

The use of HLA mapping in assessing the extent of relict landscapes is quite clear from Plate 3, and its value as a management tool can be seen when the view is enhanced by bringing in the extent of the modern commercial forestry plantations. From a map such as this it is possible to gauge the threat to the remaining relict landscapes presented by the extension of forestry plantations and, with a little additional work, to assess how much might already have been lost.

One of the other areas that has responded particularly well to HLA analysis has been the Cairngorms, and the interest in this piece of work has extended well beyond the archaeological world. Plate 4 shows the current land-use pattern around the headwaters of the Dee on the right, with the upper Spey, centred on Newtonmore and Kingussie, shown in red, on the left. Although the area is dominated by moorland, the impact of managed moorland (in purple) and commercial plantations (in green) are immediately apparent. The relict landscapes are less easy to spot than in Liddesdale but, on Plate 5, they have been isolated and set against a coloured contour background. Only a small number of prehistoric landscapes (in red) can be seen, and the majority of the relict landscapes, shown in black, are post-medieval in date. These range from townships and farmsteads to shieling sites, the latter found at heights of up to 2,700 feet on the hills to the west of Kingussie. The map shows the small-scale nature of the surviving remains of the pre-modern period in this area and, as a consequence, how vulnerable these sites are to landscape change, such as the development of forestry. But, with the aid of HLA, this type of change can be managed to reduce any potential threat.

Commercial forestry has already been mentioned in Liddesdale as a threat to the surviving relict landscapes, but it is not the only form of woodland development that conflicts with ancient landscapes. On the Mar Lodge Estate (Plate 8), HLA information was used as a management tool to minimise the impact of Scots pine regeneration (existing tree cover is shown in green) on the important post-medieval landscapes (shown in pink) in the Dee Valley and along the middle reaches of the Lui.

The examples chosen so far might have given the impression that the HLA project is concerned solely with upland environments, but the methodology is equally applicable in lowland settings where it can reveal the chronological depth concealed in the modern landscape. For example, in the north-east of Fife the vertical aerial photograph (Plate 6) of the area southward from Tayport shows the Tentsmuir forestry plantations to the east, while much of the rest of the landscape comprises post-improvement period rectilinear fields of late-eighteenth- and nineteenth-century date. As might be expected, the pattern revealed in the HLA Current Land-use Map of the same area (Plate 7) shows a rather more complex picture, and two features are of particular interest. Firstly, the rich soils of the area have been ploughed over a long period, destroying most surface traces of prehistoric and medieval settlement, but, hidden below the surface, there are some of the most extensive cropmark landscapes of early settlement and agriculture that have been found in Scotland, part of which is shown in Plate 9. Using GIS such hidden features can be displayed against the background of the modern land-use pattern.

The second point to emerge from a study of Plate 7 comes from the other end of the chronological spectrum, and reflects some of the most recent landscape developments. Through the use of modern and early maps, as well as air photos taken in the period from 1946 to 1988, we can monitor landscape change, and one of the most striking developments in this area is the erosion of the nineteenth-century agricultural landscape, as field boundaries are removed to make way for modern mechanised farming. The yellow areas define the resulting large areas of prairie fields, which are particularly prevalent to the west of Tentsmuir. In this way, the potential of HLA can be harnessed to help us to understand the dynamic nature of the man-made landscape as a whole, from earliest times to the more recent past.

First Edition Survey Project

This project, which has been funded jointly by the Royal Commission and Historic Scotland, was designed to address one of the problems arising from the development of a more broadly based landscape archaeology in the 1980s. At that time, the importance of the extensive post-medieval rural landscapes was at last recognised and due note was taken of their vulnerability to destruction by agricultural expansion and afforestation. However, these townships and farmsteads were poorly recorded in the existing national and local sites and monument records: a rapid means of filling this gap was needed.

As a solution to this problem, Scotland-wide field survey was clearly not practical and, partly in response to Historic Scotland's Medieval and Later Rural Settlement initiative, the Royal Commission decided that the most effective way to fill this information gap was to build on the data already available on the first edition of the OS 6-inch maps. Starting in Caithness and Sutherland and working southwards, the FESP team have been recording and digitising into the GIS system data on the settlements shown as deserted on the first-edition maps. The settlements are classified using the standard NMRS system and are divided, by and large, into townships, crofting townships, farmsteads, buildings and shielings. Through the GIS it is possible to show the spread of this data in the form of distribution maps, but it is also possible to interrogate the data and to select specific classes, for instance, the distribution of crofting townships.

In the course of the project some 20,000 sites have been recorded to date (the estimated total for the whole of the country is about 25,000 sites), the majority having been noted for the first time. Plate 10 shows the impact on the number of site records held in the NMRS in the northern counties. The sites in blue are those recorded by the FESP team for the first time, and those in red were already in the NMRS but were updated by FESP. The map (Plate

10) not only shows a dramatic increase in the overall numbers of sites recorded, but also the extent to which the sites already recorded relied very heavily on earlier field survey, and produced a rather biased distribution pattern. The work undertaken in the 1980s by Edinburgh University under the direction of Roger Mercer can be seen in Caithness, while the Commission's Afforestable Land surveys in Kildonan (RCAHMS, 1993a) and Skye (RCAHMS, 1993b) also stand out.

As we have already seen with the HLA data, the GIS allows data sets to be combined, and one of the most useful complements to the FESP data is the Macaulay land-use survey. The value of such overlaying is graphically demonstrated in Strathnaver (Plate 11), where the relationship of the post-medieval landscape to the modern land-use is particularly clear. The strath is sandwiched between the grey of the upland moorland, with the more intensively farmed land on the floor of the valley in apple green. Between the moorland and the better land there are patches of pasture (shown in yellow), within which the archaeology is preserved, and it is these archaeologically rich areas of former agricultural ground that are particularly vulnerable to destruction as a result of commercial afforestation.

CENTRAL SCOTLAND FOREST PROJECT

Both FESP and HLA are on-going projects designed to cover the whole of Scotland, but the third of the RCAHMS landscape-mapping projects – the Central Scotland Forest Survey – was conceived on a more modest scale and has been completed, with a summary of the results already published (RCAHMS, 1998). Rather than come last, it should, chronologically, have pride of place, as it was the testing ground for much of the work that followed in HLA and FESP.

The Central Scotland Forest Project was RCAHMS's first attempt to use early OS mapping to assess an archaeological problem – in this case the industrial archaeology of the iron, lime and coal industries in the area covered by the Central Scotland Forest. Using the first three editions of the OS 6-inch map, the remains of these industries were plotted, and in so doing the rise and fall of these industries were charted, along with that of the railway systems that supported them. Modern land reclamation and deliberate dismantling of potentially dangerous structures had already accounted for the disappearance of much of the surface remains of these industries. What we needed was a rapid means of assessing the potential of the remains, and the OS maps combined with a limited amount of field survey provided a cost effective approach.

In all some 7,000 individual sites were recorded and the data collected was used to produce a series of maps showing the state of the industries and the railway system at the date of each edition of the 6-inch surveys. The first edition, published between 1852 and 1860, recorded 480 coal and ironstone mines in operation, with a further 525 already abandoned. By the date of the second edition, between 1893 and 1897, the number of pits has been maintained, but some areas had expanded while others had been worked out. There were 967 disused pits marked, and the railway system had expanded to link the majority of the pits to the main lines. The third edition of the 6-inch map, dating to 190514, shows a reduction in the number of working pits, down to 315 from a peak of 414 on the second edition, with a corresponding shrinking of the railways, and the map also records the remains of some 1,107 abandoned mines, shafts and spoil tips. The picture is, however, is not entirely straightforward, as this was the period of maximum Scottish coal output, with production consolidated into a fewer number of larger collieries, and it was only after this period that the industry went into terminal decline.

The survey was not solely concerned with the pits themselves, but also looked at the infrastructure, such as the miners' housing, so much of which, like the pits, was demolished once the coal or iron ore reserves had been exhausted. At Haywood, Lanarkshire (Plate 12), the footings of the entire village, demolished early in the twentieth century, still survive and, rather than survey the site, the early OS maps again proved an invaluable historical source. In this case, the 1:2500 map served as the basis for a plan of the village and, through the use of digital technology it has been possible to splice together two OS maps to produce a plan of the village in its heyday (Plate 13) – a plan that would have taken many man-days to survey in the field.

The early OS maps were also used to chart the development of individual industrial complexes, such as at the oil-shale mine at Tarbrax (Plates 14 and 15), where the second and 1911 editions of the 1:2500 map show the expansion of the workings. As well as using OS maps in their own right as archaeological data, early maps can supply detail for more sophisticated archaeological surveys, such as the plan of the major early ironworks at Wilsontown (Plate 16), where ground plotting, aerial photographic survey and detail lifted from OS maps has been combined to produce a comprehensive map of the works.

Finally, although the main thrust of the Central Scotland Forest Survey was directed towards industrial remains, the wider archaeology of the area was not forgotten and, once again making the most of the new technology and early OS maps, the changing agricultural landscape of part of the area over the past one hundred and fifty years was investigated using the GIS as a base. Plate 17 maps the abandonment of farmsteads in the area between Shotts in the South and Slamannan in the north. Sites shown abandoned on the first edition of the OS 6-inch map are in black. Those abandoned since the first edition appear as dotted circles and the open circles represent farms still occupied on the latest edition. The map also shows, in dark green, the relatively large area of rig and furrow cultivation, which has been plotted using aerial photographs taken in 1945.

CONCLUSION

While this paper has given a brief introduction to three particular projects, it was also designed to draw attention to the changing nature of archaeological landscape survey and the potential of the GIS systems that are just beginning to be exploited. It is interesting to note that all three projects were joint ventures, and it is the stimulus of all the parties involved which made these advances possible. Finally, although the approach taken in all three projects was archaeologically based, the results offer a contribution towards a wider debate, which is concerned not just with history in the landscape, but the history of the landscape, with history and landscape used in their broadest senses.

ACKNOWLEDGEMENTS

This paper has drawn heavily on the work of many colleagues in the Royal Commission and Historic Scotland, and I would like to acknowledge in particular the contributions of Dr Lesley Macinnes and Dr Richard Hingley from Historic Scotland as well as Dr Piers Dixon and Steve Boyle from RCAHMS. Dr Rebecca Hughes and her colleagues in SNH have given invaluable support and encouragement for the HLA project.

REFERENCES

Dyson Bruce, L., Dixon, P., Hingley, R. and Stevenson, J. (1999). *Historic Landuse Assessment (HLA): development and potential of a technique for assessing historic landuse patterns*. Historic Scotland Research Report.

Herring, P. (1998). *Cornwall's Historic Landscape: presenting a method of Historic Landscape Character Assessment*. Cornwall Archaeological Unit and English Heritage, Truro.

RCAHMS (1993a). *Strath of Kildonan: an archaeological survey*. Edinburgh.

RCAHMS (1993b). *Waternish, Skye and Lochalsh District, Highland Region: an archaeological survey*. Edinburgh.

RCAHMS (1998). *Forts, Farms and Furnaces: archaeology in the Central Scotland Forest*. Edinburgh.

SNH (1998). *The Landscape Character of Scotland: A National Programme of Landscape Character Assessment*. SNH, Battleby.

6

History as an Aid to Understanding Peat Bogs

R. HINGLEY AND H. A. P. INGRAM

SUMMARY

The relationship is considered between ecological processes in peat bogs, the history of their formation, and their involvement in the cultural landscape.

Mires (mosses) are peat-forming systems whose soils are unusual in their structure and mode of development. Raised and blanket mires comprise associated areas of bog and fen, which engulf poorly drained terrain by upward and outward growth. Holarctic bog vegetation presents a diversity of plant-life forms having strong ecological links, especially between helophytic monocots, dwarf shrubs and *Sphagnum*, which is the chief component of bog peat. Peat deposits are like lakes with down-turned edges. They contain a mound of water which stabilises, and is stabilised by, the plant remains. The water mound is sustained by a dynamic equilibrium between surplus moisture and impeded drainage.

The strong internal integration of these systems is greatly affected by cultural activity. Burning, grazing, peat extraction, drainage and afforestation may either destroy the system by removing its peat-forming plant cover or else sustain it by preserving productive relationships between the plants and a favourable water balance.

The character of mires has meant that, as cultural landscapes, they have been used for a variety of purposes. For at least 9,000 years they have been a vital source of food, pasture and raw materials for populations living within Scotland. Settlements were sometimes constructed on or close to mires and many later prehistoric settlements in the Highlands and Islands became buried by peat after their abandonment. In prehistoric times mires appear to have had significance as special places where offerings were made to the gods and spirits. The cultural importance of mires extends into the medieval and modern period.

While using the resources provided by mires, people have modified them physically. Tree burning and cultivation may have, in some places and at some times, encouraged the commencement of peat growth. It is likely that regular burning to maintain grazing prevented regeneration and encouraged peat growth. Peat has also been cut for millennia: throughout much of human history the small scale of cutting did not have a dramatic effect on the mires of Scotland but major cutting, commencing in the late eighteenth century, has removed much of the raised mire resource. In addition, on occasions people built trackways to cross mires and settled on or around them in prehistoric and historic times.

In all these activities people have experienced, exploited and altered the mires of Scotland and continue to do so today. As sites where carbon is stored, as habitats for wildlife and as repositories of palaeoecological and archaeological information, they require conservation management, informed by recognition that they are cultural landscapes and using methods that perpetuate the historic practices of burning and grazing.

INTRODUCTION

Peat-forming wetlands are called 'mosses' colloquially and 'mires' by scientists. They function quite differently from most other terrestrial ecosystems because of peculiarities in their water relations. For most of the time the water tables in them are located very close to the soil surface. This prevents air from entering the soil pores. Consequently, the supply of oxygen to the soil is restricted, microbial activity is limited and dead plant material does not decay completely as it tends to in other terrestrial systems. This has two consequences. The undecayed portion of the plant production of the mire accumulates at the soil surface; and it is this that then becomes the parent material of the soil itself.

In other soils the parent material is the underlying rock: mineral matter that has formed within the Earth's crust and weathers on exposure to the atmosphere by a combination of physical and chemical processes. These are quite slow, so that the lower layers of a mineral soil are less altered than those at its surface. Thus soil formation in a mineral soil proceeds in an upward (acropetal) direction. In mire soils, by contrast, the new parent material produced by photosynthesis from atmospheric carbon dioxide is added at the surface and turns into soil by progressive change in a downward (basipetal) direction.

Because the differences between mire soils and mineral soils are so profound, both in their structure and in their mode of formation, the conventional terminology used for the description of mineral soils is useless for mires. Instead of trying to relate mire soil structure to the sequence of A, B and C horizons, which has been so helpful for mineral soils, we base our analyses on a simple two-layer scheme. This recognises an upper peat-forming layer called the 'acrotelm' in which virtually all the changes involved in soil formation take place; and below it a 'catotelm' (Calow, 1998), or peat deposit proper, in which any further changes are exceedingly slow. Thus, part of the carbon dioxide taken up by the vegetation is sequestered and stored by the mire.

Two basic categories of mire have been recognised, with contrasting vegetation. In fens, the soil water is enriched with mineral nutrients, whereas in bogs it is not. Fens can exist on their own but, for reasons explained later, bogs seldom, if ever, do so. Use of the generic term 'mire' is a convenient means of recognising the dual ecological nature of many peat-forming systems.

We shall concentrate mainly on two types of mire, namely 'raised mire' and 'blanket mire'. Over much of Scotland, and indeed over much of the Holarctic biogeographical realm, these support similar bog vegetation and form a similar type of peat; but whereas the formation and stability of the peat deposit is better understood for raised mires, it is from studies of blanket mire that much of our evidence about the behaviour of vegetation in response to cultural activity is derived. The larger raised mires occur in the lowlands and hitherto these have yielded more archaeological finds.

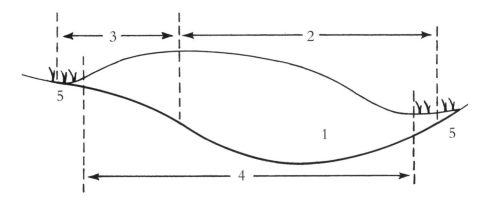

Fig. 1 Vertical section through the peat deposit of an intact raised mire that has developed by prograding to the left beyond its original lake basin (**1**) on to the adjacent slope. The thick line denotes the base of the deposit (**2**) zone of terrestrialization (**3**) zone of paludification (**4**) mire expanse (bog) (**5**) mire margin (fen).

PLANT COMMUNITY FUNCTIONS

The raised mires comprise a central expanse of bog vegetation surrounded by a narrow marginal strip of fen (Fig. 1). The bog vegetation of the mire expanse is highly characteristic. It comprises a series of components that can be classified by their life forms and taxonomic affinities (Table 1). The study of the rules by which these components are assembled is only just beginning and needs further experimental work; but sufficient evidence already exists to suggest the basic outlines of the most significant ecological interactions in these plant communities.

Table 1. Components of raised mire vegetation and their presumed ecological functions.

Taxon	Life form	Examples	Function
Gymnosperms	Shrubs, trees	*Pinus*	Shading, interception
Angiosperms	Trees	*Betula*	Shading, interception
	Dwarf shrubs	*Calluna, Erica tetralix, Empetrum*	Scaffold, shading, interception
	Insectivorous mesophytes	*Drosera*	Surface nutrition
	Helophytic monocots	*Eriophorum, Trichophorum*	Surface support
Bryophytes	Liverworts	*Odontoschisma*	Epiphytes
	Mosses	*Sphagnum*	Peat formation
Lichens	Fruticose	*Cladonia*	Erosion shield
	Foliose	*Hypogymnia*	Epiphytes

Numerous stratigraphic studies have shown that the peat formed by these communities mostly comprises the remains of bog mosses that belong to the genus *Sphagnum*. Ecologically, these are the dominant components of the community in the sense that their presence defines the habitat conditions for the majority of other plants. Several species are usually present, forming a discontinuous carpet at the mire surface. In many instances this is disposed in a mosaic of hummocks and hollows with a vertical amplitude of a few tens of centimetres and repeating itself every few metres horizontally. Conditions in the hollows tend to be wetter than on the hummocks and the various *Sphagnum* species form regular catenary arrays (Tansley, 1939, 688), in which it has been shown that some are adapted to the wetter and others to the drier habitats (Rydin, 1987).

In mires all habitats are relatively wet. This is significant for the ecology of *Sphagnum*, which is devoid of root hairs (the rhizoids found in many other mosses) and vascular tissue, and is thus unable to take up moisture from soil.

Hence, bog-forming *Sphagnum* species are always found where water tables are shallow. Suitable conditions for bog development occur where the drainage of water into the subjacent soil is impeded by a closed basin, low surface gradients or the clogging of soil pores with iron compounds (Taylor, 1983). Lake basins may be infilled with limnetic deposits and fen peat, and their central parts may then become bog-covered: a process known as 'terrestrialisation'. Bogs may also spread by the process of paludification over surrounding areas as the soil pores become clogged with iron–pan deposits (Frenzel, 1983). The growth of a raised mire that progrades beyond its terrestrialised basin involves both processes; and paludification is believed to be implicated in the spread of blanket mire over sloping terrain or plateaux (Taylor, 1993, 15).

At Walton Moss near Brampton in Cumberland (Fig. 2; Halliday, 1997), a complete series of *Sphagnum* species occurs, but there is a dearth of hummocks and hollows. The management of this site by intensive sheep-grazing ensures that the cover of dwarf shrubs is so small as to be barely detectable. This suggests that elsewhere there are strong ecological links between *Sphagnum* and the shrubs, and that these are implicated in the differentiation of hummocks and hollows. Experimenters have often observed that hummock-forming *Sphagnum* species grow more vigorously near wet surfaces (Rydin, 1993), which raises the possibility that bushes of *Calluna* (heather: the tallest of our native bog shrubs) act as scaffolds to promote local foci of upward moss growth. Furthermore, while on mineral soils *Calluna* begins to die back after about twenty years, branches that become surrounded by damp moss develop adventitious roots and are rejuvenated by a process similar to the horticulturist's layering. Thus the association between these two components promotes the stability of hummocks, while the shallower water table in hollows renders them unsuitable habitats for *Calluna*, whose roots die in anoxic conditions.

The monocotyledonous plants in these mires are mainly dwarf sedges: grass-like plants often forming tussocks. Their above-ground parts are annual leaves or shoots that tend to be less conspicuous components of the plant cover than the mosses and dwarf shrubs, except in autumn and winter when their mottled yellow, brown and russet colours may brighten the entire landscape. However, much of their plant structure occurs below the mire surface in the form of roots and rhizomes. These are physiologically adapted to withstand the anoxic conditions of soil layers that are waterlogged for long periods (Braendle & Crawford, 1999), so the sedges are said to be 'helophytie'. *Calluna*, by contrast, has a mesophytic root system without such adaptations.

Comparison with tropical peat swamps is instructive. Most of the coastal zone of Sarawak comprises a series of immense raised mires whose intact

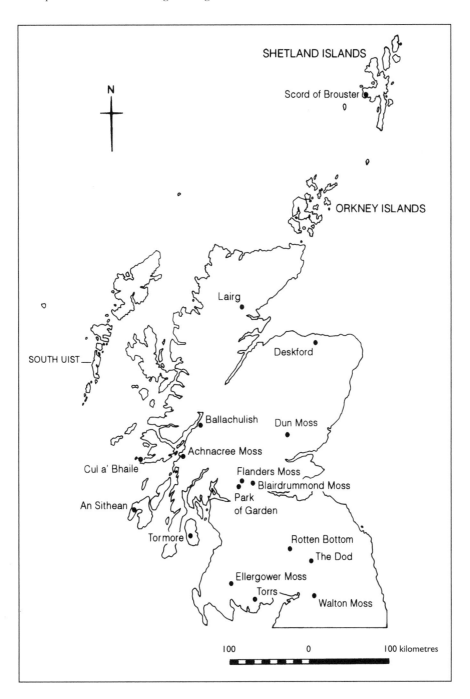

Fig. 2 Map showing locations mentioned in the text.

vegetation is a form of tropical rain forest (Anderson, 1983). The interior of the taller parts of this forest is so gloomy that low-growing components characteristic of the northern raised mires are sparse and the only sedge, *Thoracostachyum bancanum*, occurs in thin patches at intervals of some tens of metres. These mires are traversible only with great difficulty because there is no continuous living network of shallow roots and rhizomes to reinforce the surface. Thus it may be to the dwarf sedges that the frequently complex structures of the boreal raised mire surface mainly owe both their stability and their accessibility to cultural influence.

The ecological roles of other components of the open mire vegetation are less clear. Most raised mire plants are oligotrophic, that is, they have low nutrient requirements. The exceptions include mesophytes like *Drosera* (sundews). These trap and digest insects. They may, therefore, be less nutritionally constrained and may indeed add to the total stock of minerals available to the vegetation as a whole. Liverworts and foliose lichens are epiphytes which grow among, or on the branches of, other components but whose functional role is otherwise uncertain. Fruticose lichens sometimes colonise bare peat and may therefore protect the surface from erosion.

Students of vegetation in these islands have traditionally regarded our raised mires as treeless. This used indeed to be a justifiable view, since these systems only rarely supported a significant tree cover; and this was usually confined to the margin of the mire (Birse, 1980, 162). Trees cast shade on the plants beneath so their presence usually modifies the vegetation. Some of the principal peat-forming *Sphagnum* species appear to be intolerant of shade; but rigorous demonstration of this is hindered by interactions between light and water availability (Clymo & Hayward, 1982). It is also possible that deciduous species such as birches (*Betula*) may modify the mire surface by accelerating nutrient cycling through uptake and leaf fall. Their effects on hydrology are discussed below.

It will be clear from the foregoing that the vegetation of the Holarctic raised mires comprises well-integrated plant communities whose components have complementary functions (Table 1) and are linked by various ecological interactions. These are likely to be implicated in the uniform structure it presents throughout the wide geographical range over which these components occur regularly together (Fig. 3).

HYDROLOGY AND DRAINAGE

Because shallow water tables play so important a part in the ecology of raised mires, their ecohydrology has received close scientific attention (for example, Romanov, 1968; Ivanov, 1981; Ingram, 1987, 1992).

Raised mires are fed by water along two routes. Telluric water reaches the mire from the mineral soils of its surroundings and is therefore enriched by mineral nutrients dissolved from these soils. Meteoric water arrives in the form of atmospheric precipitation. This is poor in nutrients and gives most of the vegetation of these mires its oligotrophic character. Most terrestrial ecosystems outwith the Arid Zone are fed by a combination of telluric and meteoric water. In a raised mire, however, the influence of telluric water is confined to the low-lying marginal strip, leaving the central mire expanse, which is higher and usually accounts for most of the surface area, to be fed by meteoric water alone. Hence, in these mires there tends to be a separation of areas with oligotrophic bog vegetation, developed under the influence of exclusively meteoric water, from areas in which the predominating telluric influence is shown by the presence of eutrophic fen vegetation with a

Fig. 3 Spatial relationships of some components of treeless raised mire vegetation, showing relative positions of buds (•), roots and shoots. (**1**) *Calluna vulgaris* (**2**) *Drosera anglica* (**3**) *Eriophorum vaginatum* (**4**) *Odontoschisma sphagni* (**5**) *Sphagnum magellanicum* (stems with side branches forming tufts at their apices) (**6**) *Cladonia* (2 species) (**7**) *Hypogymnia physodes*.

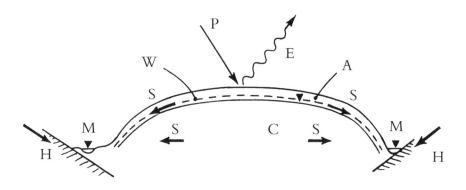

Fig. 4 Vertical section through a raised mire to illustrate its water relations.
A, acrotelm; **C**, catotelm; **H**, surrounding hill slopes; **M**, mire margin; **W**, water table.
Water levels are marked (▼). Arrows denote fluxes of water: **E**, evapotranspiration;
P, precipitation; **S**, seepage.

relatively high nutrient requirement. This separation, often with a clear demarcation along the 'mineral soil water limit' (Sjörs, 1948), is a characteristic that raised mires owe to their gross morphology (Fig. 1).

Raised mires are so called from the convexity of their surfaces: the centre is always higher than the edge. This controls the associated fluxes of soil water (Fig. 4). In the mire expanse, water of meteoric origin drains centrifugally towards the margin. Telluric water from the surroundings also drains towards the margin, but centripetally. Water from the margin cannot ascend on to the expanse against gravity: hence the clear separation between the eutrophic fen vegetation of the margin and the oligotrophic bog vegetation of the expanse. Moreover the nutrient load which the mineral soil water contributes to the margin ensures that it remains lower than the expanse because the nutrients accelerate decay and retard the accumulation of peat (Gilbert, Amblard, Bourdier & Francez, 1998).

Plant growth on the mire expanse drives the accumulation of a convex mound of peat. This forms the catotelm. In an intact mire it is perennially waterlogged, so the mound of peat is co-extensive with a mound of water. Since the material of the catotelm comprises more than 90 per cent water the mire expanse is in reality a strange kind of lake, traversible thanks only to its vegetation, and with a surface that slopes down towards its shores.

Such ground-water mounds are phenomena familiar to engineers and geophysicists. They develop wherever the free flow of water is impeded by the porous medium through which it drains. In raised mires that medium is the peat of the catotelm itself. Thus, just as the water mound stabilises the peat by excluding oxygen and retarding decay, so the peat stabilises the water mound by impeding centrifugal flow. So strong is their mutual dependence that the shape of the water mound determines the shape of the catotelm, and hence the gross morphology of the mire.

The centrifugal flow of water is impeded because the peat in the catotelm is rather impermeable to water: it is said to possess a low hydraulic conductivity. This prevents the collapse of the water mound so long as the slow radial discharge of seeping water is made good by fresh supplies. The availability of these is determined by the water balance of the mire (Fig. 4).

Inputs of water arrive at the surface as atmospheric precipitation only, so that they are relatively easy to measure. A certain fraction of this is lost to the atmosphere by evaporation from wet surfaces or transpiration from the leaves of plants, the combination of these two processes being termed 'evapotranspiration'. The size of this fraction depends on season and climate, one consequence being that bogs cannot develop in regions where the fraction exceeds unity, indicating a climate under which the mean annual total evapotranspiration is greater than the mean annual total precipitation. The process of evapotranspiration is physically complex and its rate also depends on the stature of the vegetation. Short vegetation reduces the rate because it has little capacity for detaining moisture on leaves and twigs and it also presents a smooth upper surface that causes little turbulence in adjacent air currents. However, tall vegetation, extensively wetted by rainfall and with a rough foliage canopy that promotes vigorous turbulence and rapid mixing in the lowest layer of the atmosphere, increases the rate of evaporative water loss (Oke, 1987).

The water remaining after evapotranspiration finds its way into the soil. Most of it is stored temporarily in the acrotelm, through which it eventually seeps away towards the mire margin. Although this upper layer of soil is very thin, it has a much higher hydraulic conductivity than the catotelm (Romanov, 1968; Ingram & Bragg, 1984) and is thus able to disperse surplus storm water in a manner harmless to the *Sphagnum* mosses, whose lack of anchorage renders them vulnerable to sheet erosion. The small amount of water remaining descends into the catotelm where it recharges the ground-water mound. It has been suggested for Dun Moss (Ingram, 1982) that this amount may be estimated as the annual surplus remaining after evapotranspiration at the end of the driest year through which the mire survives. Although amounting to as little as 530mm, this is the water that sustains the dynamic equilibrium between recharge and catotelm discharge.

Geophysical considerations predict that the sectional profile of the water mound and catotelm should approximate to a half ellipse with a horizontal major axis (Ingram, 1982): a hypothesis tested (Fig. 2) at Dun Moss in Perthshire and (by R. S. Clymo and P. D. Hulme) at Ellergower Moss in

Dumfries-shire (Ingram, 1987). Three-dimensional models are available for raised mires situated in parallel-sided troughs or with circular or elliptical margins (Ingram, 1992). All the models indicate that taller raised mires containing taller ground-water mounds will be found in circumstances that promote greater moisture surplus and hence greater recharge, or where discharge is impeded because catotelms have lower hydraulic conductivities.

CONTEMPORARY HUMAN INFLUENCE

As with their soils and vegetation, so with their water relations, the raised mires appear to present a very high degree of integration. In space, this extends both vertically and horizontally, and it encompasses both biological and geophysical attributes. How are the strong internal links that govern these systems affected by mankind? What part has human influence played in moulding their development? Does it still operate? Might it be changing in nature or extent? And how might the mires themselves change in response? These are not just academic questions. The very survival of the Holarctic raised mires may depend upon the answers (Ingram, 1997). The main cultural influences have been burning, grazing, drainage and peat extraction.

BURNING

Under the designation *muirburn* this is widely practised in Scotland as a method of managing unimproved pasture and grouse moors in which *Calluna* and other dwarf shrubs are important components of the plant cover. The primary objective is to enhance livestock productivity by improving the forage quality and palatability of the vegetation to grazing animals, so that burning and grazing are associated aspects of the same system of pasture management.

Dry, woody vegetation burns readily once ignited, but the effect of the fire depends on circumstances. Wind is a critical factor. Fire tends to travel towards unburned fuel. If this lies downwind, the fire and the wind move in the same direction so temperatures are relatively low and the flames travel rapidly as a head fire, mainly through the canopy of foliage and twigs. If it lies upwind, however, the fire travels slowly and has an abundant supply of oxygen, so that high temperatures are generated, plant litter rapidly dries out and structures close to the ground surface are destroyed.

The effect of burning varies with the plant. Plant growth is renewed from buds that are differently situated depending on the growth form. On the raised mire expanse the dwarf shrubs produce buds at the tips of the shoots within the canopy. A head fire destroys these but leaves the shoot bases intact to regenerate by the activation of dormant buds. New leafy shoots may then appear within months of burning and the main effect is greatly to shorten the stature of the plant. A slow hot fire, travelling towards the wind, destroys the shoot bases as well as the canopy. The shrubs then die and are replaced by the germination and establishment of seeds: a slower process, but one that may actually be accelerated on the seed bed left by a destructive fire. The effect on helophytic monocots is somewhat different. In these, the only perennial structure is a rhizome, bearing buds at or just below the soil surface. New leaves, aerial shoots and roots are produced, often in close proximity, annually or at shorter intervals. Only extremely slow hot fires, capable of destroying the acrotelm itself, are likely to kill these plants. Less severe burning only affects the architecture of the aerial organs for the current growing season at most. *Sphagnum* mosses may be unaffected by rapidly travelling head fires but, despite their great capacity to retain moisture, they are very sensitive to slow hot ones.

Muirburn as a management tool is generally applied to treeless hill grazings and its affect on trees is therefore not at the front of the practitioner's mind. Nevertheless, this effect is of the utmost importance since, together with grazing, it is chiefly responsible for maintaining the vegetation in a treeless condition and thus for sustaining the mixture of plants with other life forms, which is the object of management. Being relatively slow to establish from seed and grow, trees are especially sensitive to fire, and conifers in particular lack the capacity to regenerate from dormant lateral buds: a prominent feature of angiosperm biology. Tree establishment may also be affected by seed-bed creation following fire, but we know of little evidence for the importance of this on raised mires. It is, however, possible that belts of trees on the sloping edge of the mire expanse may owe their origin partly to this cause, since muirburn is more often carried out on this part of the mire than elsewhere.

GRAZING

Since the object of muirburn is usually the improvement of forage or habitat quality for farming or sporting purposes, it is difficult in practice to justify distinguishing the ecological effects of burning and grazing. Moreover, moorland areas that are managed primarily for grouse shooting tend to be used also as pasture for sheep and cattle, and at the time of writing many of those in or near the Scottish Highlands are increasingly affected by grazing red deer, whose total population appears to have doubled since the early 1900s and is thought to be larger now than at any time since the mid- to late-eighteenth century (Staines, Balharry & Welch, 1995).

Foraging by grouse has little direct effect on vegetation. Their main source of food is the young shoots of heather, *Calluna vulgaris*, but the offtake is small in relation to annual shoot production (Gimingham, 1972, 182). Their chief effect is indirect, arising from the need for managers to provide a patchy environment in which tall, dense heather bushes, providing cover for nests and chicks, are juxtaposed with young regrowth, providing a high density of food. Burning frequency varies with the rate of heather growth, which is governed by climate, but roughly a decade often elapses between fires, and moorlands with smaller patches sustain higher grouse populations.

Mammalian herbivores have more direct effects. Red deer can convert heather-dominated moorland to grass dominance (Staines *et al.,* 1995). Sheep especially are known to graze vegetation selectively, resulting in suppression of *Calluna* (Rawes & Hobbs, 1979), and also seasonally, eating the tender leaf and stem bases ('scallions') of the helophytes which provide a valuable source of phosphorus and protein in early spring when little other forage is available (Thomas & Trinder, 1947). Trees are especially vulnerable and grazing suppresses scrub colonisation between successive muirburns. On the other hand, *Sphagnum* is generally ignored. Mammals also affect the mire surface by trampling. While this may occasionally destroy the surface (see later comments on trackways), it has been noticed that regular routes, such as the narrow ridges separating suites of pools (*dubh lochans*) in the central parts of some large mires, are surprisingly firm, which may be due to the compacting effect of frequently passing feet.

At the time of writing a system of agricultural subsidy based on headage has caused an increase in stocking rates on many upland pasture ranges that include areas of blanket bog. The review by Hulme & Birnie (1997) reflects current concerns about the effect of this by concentrating on over-grazing and the mire degradation that results. But these authors acknowledge that low-intensity grazing is a 'natural' feature of these systems and that domestic livestock may simply have replaced earlier populations of large wild herbivores.

DRAINAGE

The availability of suitable equipment and petroleum-derived energy to drag it has in recent decades caused a great increase in the digging of drains across mires: an activity that was formerly prohibitively laborious (Stewart & Lance, 1983). The purpose of this is to ameliorate conditions, making the surface more commercially productive, either for livestock forage or for timber, and often facilitating the introduction of plants that do not naturally grow on mires and require an input of artificial fertilisers. Drainage for afforestation is generally followed by the development of deep cracks below the drains as the peat dries out (Pyatt & John, 1989, 695-6) because the tree crop alters the water balance.

Thus, burning and grazing have subtle but profound effects on mires. The current spread of trees across bog surfaces throughout NW Europe has coincided with a decline in pastoralism. Since both processes destroy trees, the suggestion of causality cannot lightly be dismissed. Even where trees do not invade, the abandonment of pastoralism may greatly alter the ecology of the mire surface. Walton Moss (Fig. 2) is used as a common grazing and has a wet surface; but on many other raised mires the vegetation has lately become dominated by tall moribund *Calluna* bushes, while *Sphagnum* growth has been suppressed and the surface is becoming drier. This suggests that burning and grazing play a crucial role in maintaining the delicate relationship between these two components of bog vegetation. Since tall vegetation with an uneven canopy promotes evapotranspiration, it is likely that the suppression of trees also promotes a water balance that favours peat accumulation.

PEAT EXTRACTION

Long practised as means of obtaining cheap domestic fuel, peat-digging has also been mechanised in recent decades. While domestic activities have generally concentrated on the accessible marginal parts of mires, modern machinery enables the whole surface to be worked simultaneously after preliminary drainage. The product has served in Ireland as fuel for power stations. In Britain most of it has been used in horticulture as a soil conditioner or compost base.

Drainage and peat extraction have great effects on the hydrology of mires. Drainage lowers the water table, rendering the surface an unsuitable habitat for peat-forming *Sphagnum*, interrupting the accumulation of peat and causing the catotelm to shrink and crack (Ingram, 1992, 71). Local peat extraction from the edge of a mire also lowers the water table by shortening the base of the water mound (Bragg, Brown & Ingram, 1991), with similar consequences. Commercial peat-working often begins with removal of the entire acrotelm and vegetation, and therefore causes the most profound changes almost instantaneously. The changes following afforestation are also profound, creating a new plant cover, but may take a few decades to be completed.

HISTORY OF HUMAN INFLUENCE

The human input into the management of mires in the recent past and present has already been discussed. We turn at this point to the past uses to which they have been put by people and to their significance as cultural landscapes. Cultural landscapes reflect the interaction between people and their environment over space and time (Plachter & Rossler, 1995, 15). In human terms, these landscapes are never inert as people engage with them, rework them, appropriate and contest them (Bender, 1993, 3). They are complex phenomena with both tangible and intangible aspects (Plachter & Rossler, 1995, 15).

The tangible impact of humans on the cultural landscapes of mires includes physical impacts (for instance, the clearing of trees from the Neolithic onward and the digging of peat throughout history), while the intangible aspects relate to ideas and attitudes (for instance, beliefs in peatlands as special places both in the past and in the present). Mires have developed their present form partly as a result of the interaction of people with their environment. This interaction has resulted from the uses to which mires have been put in the past and the effect of these uses upon mires. Even the act of preserving the mire out of a respect for its importance is a cultural act of an intangible type, as are the tangible acts undertaken to improve the condition of many mires in recent years, including damming and rewatering. Thus, various tangible and intangible actions have had significant impacts upon the nature of Scottish mires through time.

The exact role of human activity with regard to the early development of mires remains unclear and the question of whether people helped to create the circumstances under which they first formed is discussed below. Nevertheless, even if the environmental explanation for mire formation is pushed to its extreme and it is argued that human activity had no part in helping to create the correct environmental circumstances, mires have still constituted cultural landscapes since people first encountered them. Because of the natural resources which mires provide, they will have taken on a role as an element of the social landscape since their formation or since the arrival of people, whichever came first.

We will now turn to a general consideration of the history of human involvement with mires, considering first whether people helped to create the circumstances under which mires first started to develop; then how they have been exploited; and finally their role as special, spiritual landscapes.

MIRE CREATION: HUMAN INVOLVEMENT?

The blanket mires of Scotland originated at differing times from as early as *c.*8500 BC, according to calibrated radiocarbon dates (Edwards & Whittington, 1997, 81). It is likely that a continuous, but not necessarily constant, process of peat inception and spread has been in operation across much of Scotland since this time. In general terms, climatic change may have played a major role in the process of peat development, with cooling temperatures and/or increased rainfall creating the conditions for peat growth, although insufficient evidence is available to substantiate this suggestion (*Ibid.*).

It has been proposed by some researchers that human activity has played a major part in the inception of blanket peat formation over much of the uplands of Scotland, although the level of its contribution to the process is a contentious issue (for a review of earlier work, see Moore, 1993; for a recent review see Thompson & Miles, 1995, 370-1). One interpretation views the activities of prehistoric people as having played a major part in the origin of mires through forest clearance and the resultant modification of upland hydrology. People have been disturbing the natural tree canopy since the Mesolithic era, although the disturbance is unlikely to have had a large effect on the natural distribution of plant communities this early: see Tipping (1994, 15-16) for a summary of earlier work. From the Neolithic period onward the impact on tree-cover became far more dramatic, although tree clearance appears to have been gradual, with periods of regeneration. This led to a situation in which, by the early centuries AD, large areas of Scotland had been subjected to considerable deforestation (*Ibid.*, 32-7). The burning of trees sometimes appears to have been a mechanism by which clearance was induced, either by burning *in situ* or by the burning of trees which had already been felled (*Ibid.*, 36), while grazing was also an important mechanism of tree clearance.

Research has indicated that the addition of charcoal to the soil through the burning of vegetation can have an effect in reducing its porosity and helping to retain water in the soil (Mallik, Gimingham & Rahman, 1984). The removal of tree-cover may therefore have had a major impact on the development of mires. A problem with this view is that the growth of blanket peat during prehistory is itself regarded as a likely cause of the decline in tree-cover, and whether the clearing of trees caused the growth of mires, or the spread of mires caused the decline of trees, is unclear (Tipping, 1994, 15). Evidence for the past burning of vegetation is common in Scotland (see below) and future study may help to investigate in greater detail the human impact on tree-cover and the influence of this on mire formation.

Evidence also exists that prehistoric ploughing could have had the effect of forming an iron pan which then impeded drainage (Case, Dimbleby, Mitchell, Morrison & Proudfoot, 1969; Taylor & Smith, 1972), thus inducing mire development by paludification. More recent work, however, suggests that soil-disturbance by cultivation can prevent the development of surface-water gleying and hence blanket peat accumulation (Carter, 1998, 154). Cultivation may therefore have had two influences: promoting conditions favourable to peat growth while semi-permanently preventing its initiation until the episode of cultivation had ended (*Ibid.*).

The evidence from research about the effects of burning and cultivation on soils may indicate that a process occurred in which the clearance of trees, cultivation and the subsequent abandonment of cultivated areas led to the development of blanket peat across much of the uplands of Scotland (Moore, 1993). It is fairly common to find prehistoric settlements and field systems buried under blanket peat and other mires, and it has been argued by some that this helps to provide a link between cultivation, soil depletion and the inception of peat formation. Relevant archaeological sites (Fig. 2) range from the Scord of Brouster (Shetland), to sites in Argyll (including Achnacree Moss) and nearby islands (Cul a'Bhaile, Jura; An Sithean, Islay; and Tormore, Arran) to Lairg in Sutherland (Davidson & Carter, 1997, 57; McCullagh & Tipping, 1998; Carter, 1998; see also the evidence for buried landscapes discussed by Hingley, Ashmore, Clarke & Sheridan, 1999). Several of these sites show buried podsols in areas now covered by peat or peaty podsols and radiocarbon dates suggest that peat inception began in the first millennium BC or first millennium AD (Davidson & Carter, 1997, 57; see also Whittington & Edwards 1997, 18).

Often the lack of closely dated complete soil profiles prevents a detailed consideration of the balance of natural and cultural influences on the formation of peat on these prehistoric sites (Carter 1998, 154). There is a considerable debate about whether the beginning of peat development was a result of gleying, itself caused by arable farming, or whether the whole process was driven by environmental change. In fact, the period 2650–2700 BC appears to be marked by increased precipitation and/or a decline in temperature (Barber, 1982); and the abandonment of farming in upland areas might have resulted from ecological stress caused by a deteriorating environment: this deterioration also resulting in increased peat formation.

In conclusion, although archaeological evidence from both sides of the Atlantic may support the association between tree-felling/ploughing and the consequent development of blanket peat over large areas (Moore, 1993), the human contribution to the start of mire formation is likely to have been, at most, only one in a range of causes. It is possible that climatic and other natural processes may have been more significant in the development of peat than cultural influences.

RESOURCE EXPLOITATION IN THE PAST

Further detailed research on individual sites may shed more light on the relationship between climate, natural burning, animal grazing and human activity in the formation of Scottish mires. The complex balance between the various contributory factors is likely to mean that any attempt at a definitive monocausal explanation is untenable. Yet even if the process of bog initiation over the whole of Scotland is eventually shown to be entirely natural, this will not invalidate the conclusion that these mires are essentially part of the cultural landscape. For it is probable that people have incorporated mires into their settled surroundings and in so doing have made full use of their resources since the first human use of the Scottish landscape.

Once peat began to grow it became part of the social environment of the people who lived around the mire and of those who visited it. Peat growth occurred in and around the settled landscapes of the prehistoric and later occupants of Scotland, and bogs would have been used for a wide range of purposes throughout history. We have considered above the current effects of a range of activities: burning, grazing, draining and peat extraction. In the past, these acts of mire management (or exploitation) will have been bound up with a changing range of human attitudes to the peatlands. We now consider the archaeological evidence both for these and other activities.

The use of mires for a wide variety of purposes is reflected in the evidence for human artefacts and structures in the wetlands of Scotland. An archaeological database of finds from Scottish wetlands, which has been created recently (Clarke, 1997; Ellis, 1999a), contains approximately 6,500 entries of archaeological sites, artefacts and ecofacts. Recoveries listed vary from the Mesolithic to the post-medieval period and include settlements, stray finds, metal hoards, organic artefacts and bog bodies. The range and diversity of records reflects the domestic and subsistence importance of wetland areas to bygone generations, and also alludes to their use as places of spiritual or ceremonial significance as well as their role as cultural landscapes (Hingley, Ashmore, Clarke & Sheridan, 1999). The database further illustrates the archaeological potential of wetlands, resulting from the enhanced preservation of organic materials in these contexts. The range of archaeological materials found in mires has been considered elsewhere (Clarke, 1997 and Ellis, 1999a).

HUNTING

Mires provide forage both for wild game and for domesticated mammalian herbivores. It is indeed likely that their value as a source of forage may first have been recognised by hunters, and that their pastoral use followed later. Mires may well have been used for hunting throughout human history. Foraging game might have attracted Mesolithic, Neolithic and later people on to the peat to hunt. Burning may also have been employed to increase the number of animals that a piece of land could support, thus resulting in peat growth in peat-free areas. The earliest bow known from the British Isles, found in a mire at Rotten Bottom (Fig. 2), in Dumfriesshire (dated by radiocarbon to *c*.4040-3640 BC : Sheridan, 1996), may have been carried during one of these hunting expeditions. Animals were hunted in Scotland down to the present century and, as more of the landscape was used for arable and pasture, wild animals will have been driven in increasing numbers into marginal areas, including mires. Over the past 150 years, many upland heaths and moorlands have been managed by estates to encourage the raising and cropping of red grouse for pleasure and for profit; these areas are now of great nature conservation interest.

GRAZING

Peatlands would also have been a major resource for people from the Neolithic onwards because they provided grazing for livestock. Throughout prehistoric, medieval and post-medieval times, human communities were vitally dependent on their animals, which usually formed part of a mixed-farming economy. In post-medieval times mires have been particularly important in providing a source of forage for animals over the winter (Smout, 1997).

Widespread evidence exists for charcoal within the peat profile in mires that have been examined through palynology. Charcoal occurs throughout the profile in many of the mires examined as part of the English Heritage-funded North-West Wetlands Survey in north-western England (Colin Wells *pers. comm.*). It has also been found, for instance, in the archaeological evaluation of the bog at North Ballachulish (Ciara Clarke *pers. comm.*) and in a survey of wet heath development on South Uist (Edwards, Whittington & Hirons, 1995), and its occurrence is to be expected elsewhere (see additional references in Ingram, 1997, 160). The significance of these observations is that, as has been argued above, at the same time that the burning of heather prevents woodland regeneration over the peat, it enhances its grazing potential (Ingram, 1997, 160). We suggest that the evidence for burning in the peat profile mainly records generations upon generations of human management of peat bogs for grazing by animals. Indeed, the proximity of homestead moats in the Carse of Stirling to Offerance Moss and Flanders Moss (Fig. 2) suggest that these lowland raised mires were grazed by domestic livestock in the Dark Ages; and a similar conclusion for the suite of upland raised mires (including Dun Moss: Fig. 2) in the Forest of Alyth seems inescapable in view of the remarkably dense concentration of Neolithic and subsequent settlement remains by which they are surrounded (RCAHMS, 1990).

EXPLOITATION OF OTHER PEAT RESOURCES

In addition to hunting and grazing, mires would have been used as a source of wild fruits and other foodstuffs. Peat is also likely to have represented an important fuel throughout prehistoric times and peat-cutting probably occurred from the earliest times. At The Dod (Fig. 2) in the Scottish Borders, pollen analysis has indicated a missing section of 3,000 years in late Flandrian peat deposits and the inversion of other deposits; Innes & Shennan (1991) have suggested that this may be a result of peat-cutting in antiquity. Tipping has proposed peat cutting in the Bowmont Valley (Borders) in the late Iron Age (*pers. comm.*). Digging tools, which could have been used for cutting peat, have been found in ironwork hoards dating to the first to second century AD in southern Scotland (Rees, 1979), while the fact that most technical terms associated with peat-cutting in Orkney are Norse may indicate the importance of this resource to people at this time (Fenton, 1970). Evidently, peat has remained an important source of fuel until the present day across much of the Highlands and Islands, and this was also true in the lowlands well into the post-medieval period (Grant, 1961, 199-201). Since the morphology of a mire is hydrologically controlled, peat cutting in one place is likely to have affected development of the system as a whole (Bragg, Brown & Ingram, 1981). Where it results in draw-down of the water table and air entry, oxidisation of plant remains ensues. This, together with the burning of the extracted peat, releases stored carbon, thus adding to the carbon dioxide content of the atmosphere.

ACCESS TO MIRE RESOURCES

Wooden trackways of prehistoric and later date are fairly common archaeological discoveries across England and Ireland (for a general discussion, see Coles & Coles, 1989, 151-72; for some of the recent Irish discoveries, see

Raftery, 1996). The act of constructing a trackway was intended to make passage across a mire easier, but it may also on occasions have been intended to protect the surface vegetation of the mire which is destroyed by frequent trampling. This vegetation supports the mire surface and so paths across mires that are in regular use quickly degenerate. The surface of the track can be improved by adding a layer of brushwood and small roundwood derived from stems and roots. The construction of a wooden trackway might represent an attempt by a human community to manage the surface of a mire to ensure its survival in a stable state. This technique has been widely employed in the building of minor roads in the Highlands of Scotland and continues today, but with polypropylene mesh giving the tensile strength formerly provided by forest products.

Prehistoric trackways appear from available information to have been rare in Scotland, although at least four examples were found during the clearing of Blairdrummond Moss and Flanders Moss (Fig. 2) in the eighteenth and nineteenth centuries (Clarke, 1997; Ellis, 1999b) and a possible example is known in Grampian (Ellis, 1999b). During archaeological evaluation work, a wooden platform has been rediscovered at Park of Garden (Fig. 2) close to the south-west edge of Flanders Moss and this may have assisted access to the bog (Ellis, 1998, 1999b and 1999c). Four individual wooden wheels were found in Blairdrummond Moss during its clearance and one survives in the National Museums and has been dated to *c*.1255–815 BC (Sheridan, 1996). This may demonstrate that wheeled transport was used within the bogs during the later part of the Bronze Age. Trackways have been shown by archaeological work to have been very common in the Somerset Levels and in areas of Ireland, and it is likely that numerous trackways existed to transport people and stock through and into the bogs of Scotland. The prehistoric trackways may have been used for transport across peatlands and the hunting of wild animals, but would also have allowed readier use of the other resources of the peat and would have served to make areas of mire available for grazing by domestic livestock.

ATTITUDES TO PEAT: MIRES AS SPECIAL PLACES

Another property of mires, in prehistory and increasingly in the present, is their spiritual role as special places: a role which may often have led to distinct forms of management and use. Such spiritual attitudes to the landscape will have affected the ways in which people used the resources that it provided.

Throughout prehistory and the early historical period various distinctive objects were placed in Scottish mires and wetlands, including weapons, defensive armour and bog butter (Clarke, 1997; Hunter, 1997). The most remarkable of these objects include impressive pieces of later prehistoric metalwork such as the Torrs pony cap and the Deskford carnyx (Fig. 2), possibly placed in the mire as an offering to the gods (Hunter, 1997). Other finds include discoveries of bog butter (a product derived from animal fat) contained in wooden vessels that were placed in Scottish mires from at least the third century AD and probably earlier (Earwood, 1997, 27). This, too, may have formed an offering to the gods, although it has also been suggested that the butter was left in peat to improve its flavour (see Hingley, 1998, 50).

The Scottish evidence forms part of a general pattern in Iron Age Europe of the deposition of various objects in rivers, lakes and wetlands (Green, 1993). It may be that objects were deposited as offerings to the gods in such contexts partly because they could not be easily located, stolen or violated (*Ibid.*). It has also been suggested that people in the past were aware of the property of peat as a preserver of organic materials. Organic objects may have been placed in peat and retrieved as preserved objects at a later time. If so, later prehistoric people may have placed both organic objects and human bodies in mires because of ideas about life-cycles and regeneration (Finn, 1999 and *pers. comm.*). Such ideas might well be bound up with the desire to offer materials to the gods to influence the situation of people.

Human bodies of prehistoric date have often been found in mires across northern Europe, for example 'Lindow Man' in Cheshire (Stead, Bourke & Brothwell, 1986). No modern discoveries of prehistoric bog bodies have been made in Scotland, although bodies of post-medieval date have been found in several mires in the past (Turner & Briggs, 1986; Turner & Scaife, 1995). Prehistoric bodies may be linked with ideas about the spiritual nature of the bog (Ross, 1986), while the post-medieval period finds may often have been individuals who became lost in the mire, or were deliberately buried there for unknown reasons.

Another major find was the Ballachulish figure, discovered in a moss during the late nineteenth century. This life-sized wooden naked female figure has been dated to around 700 BC using radiocarbon dating, and the findspot was the location for the deposition of a range of objects during later prehistory. Recent archaeological evaluation has suggested that Ballachulish Moss (Fig. 2) is likely to have been a major focus for ritual activity in later prehistory (Hingley, Ashmore, Clarke & Sheridan, 1999), possibly comparable to several major later prehistoric sites including Llyn Cerrig Bach in Wales and Nydam in Denmark (Coles & Coles, 1995, 132). It seems likely that a variety of other sites of similar importance survives undiscovered within Scotland (Hingley, 1998, 4951).

These prehistoric finds suggest that Scottish mires and wetlands were thought of as special places by prehistoric people: possibly as places in which the gods could be contacted and petitioned (Hingley, 1998). The disappearance of former agricultural land under peatlands (see above) might have been associated in the later prehistoric mind with the idea of an environmental crisis: the slow invasion of bog on to parts of the landscape which were once cultivated or occupied by the ancestors (Hingley, 1995, 188). This might have created a view of bogs as an encroaching powerful problem in the later prehistoric mind. On the other hand, the value of mires as sources of raw materials and grazing areas for stock may also have resulted in a positive image of these places, as was the case in post-medieval Scotland (see below). Perhaps the objects which were left for the gods during prehistory may demonstrate attempts by individual people and communities to seek the help of divine spirits in a variety of activities ranging from every-day agricultural and domestic tasks to full-scale war.

Professor Smout has reviewed how positive views existed from 1630 to 1730 of mires as sources of fodder and raw materials and this is probably typical of the views of people to bogs throughout much of human history. The darker side of the image of bogs, as places in which the gods and spirits could be contacted and petitioned, may have survived well into Christian times. Various finds of early medieval, medieval and post-medieval date occur in Scottish bogs and suggest that the advent of Christianity did not drive out all pre-existing beliefs. This positive view gave way in the age of the agricultural improvers to the idea that boglands were waste areas ripe for exploitation (Smout, 1997). Detailed historical sources exist for the large-scale clearance of some areas of peat during the eighteenth and nineteenth centuries (Mackay forthcoming), and peat has been exploited on a fairly large scale since this time. During the twentieth century, however, the public attitude gradually swung back towards a regard for mires as special places: for their significance for wildlife conservation rather than for ritual or supernatural beliefs. Increasingly, they are also being recognised for their role as repositories of palaeoecological and archaeological evidence. These ideas define the ways in which mires can be 'exploited' by people today and their protection as a valuable resource for the future is also informed in this way. On the other hand, effective prescriptions for conserving the resource will not emerge unless the role of people in their past development is recognised. Mires, like other cultural landscapes, will only survive if we continue to use them in appropriate ways that respect their long cultural history.

Acknowledgements

The authors are grateful to Professors John and Bryony Coles and Professor Christopher Smout for their general encouragement; also to Dr David Breeze, Dr Peter Hulme, Dr Lesley Macinnes, Dr Alison Sheridan, Dr

Richard Tipping, Christina Unwin and Dr Berwyn Williams for comments and advice. Fig. 2 was drawn by Christina Unwin and the other illustrations are by Mary Benstead. Ros Wakefield kindly checked the manuscript for inconsistencies.

Many of the ideas mentioned earlier in the chapter were developed while HAPI was working in the Department of Biological Sciences, University of Dundee, while much of the research for the latter part was conducted while RH was an Inspector of Ancient Monuments with Historic Scotland.

REFERENCES

Anderson, J A R, (1983). The tropical peat swamps of western Malesia. In Gore, A J P (ed) *Mires: Swamp, Bog Fen and Moor*, **B**, 181-199. Elsevier, Amsterdam.

Barber, K E (1982). Peat-bog stratigraphy as a proxy climatic record. In Harding, A (ed) *Climatic Change in Later Prehistory*, 103-13. Edinburgh University Press, Edinburgh.

Bender, B (1993). Landscapes – meaning and action. In Bender, B (ed) *Landscape: Politics and Perspectives*, 118. Berg, Oxford.

Birse, E L (1980). *Plant Communities of Scotland: a Preliminary Phytocoenonia*. Macaulay Institute, Aberdeen.

Braendle, R & Crawford, R M M (1999). Plants as amphibians. *Perspectives in Plant Ecology, Evolution and Systematics*, **2**, 56-78.

Bragg, O M, Brown, J M B & Ingram, H A P (1991). Modelling the ecohydrological consequences of peat extraction from a Scottish raised mire. In Nachtnebel, H P & Kovar, K (eds) *Hydrological Basis of Ecologically Sound Management of Soil and Groundwater*, 13-22. International Association of Hydrological Sciences, Wallingford.

Calow, P (1998). *The Encyclopedia of Ecology & Environmental Management*. Blackwell Science, Oxford.

Carter, S (1998). Palaeopedology. In McCullagh, R & Tipping, R (eds) *The Lairg Project 1988-1996: The Evolution of an Archaeological Landscape in Northern Scotland*, 150-5. Scottish Trust for Archaeological Research, Monograph **3**, Edinburgh.

Case, H J, Dimbleby, G W, Mitchell, G F, Morrison, M E S & Proudfoot, V B (1969). Land use in Goodland Township, Co. Antrim, from Neolithic times until today. *Journal of the Royal Society of Antiquaries of Ireland* **99**, 39-53.

Clarke, C (1997). *Archaeological Database for the Scottish Wetlands*. Unpublished report produced for Historic Scotland, Centre for Field Archaeology Report No.298, Edinburgh.

Clymo, R S & Hayward, P M (1982). The ecology of *Sphagnum*. In Smith, A J E (ed) *Bryophyte Ecology*, 229-289. Chapman & Hall, London.

Coles, B & Coles, J (1989). *People of the Wetlands: Bog Bodies and Lake Dwellers*. Thames & Hudson, London.

Coles, J & Coles, B (1995). *Enlarging the Past: the Contribution of Wetland Archaeology*. Society of Antiquaries of Scotland, Edinburgh.

Davidson, D A & Carter, S P (1997). Soils and their evolution. In Edwards, K. J. & Ralston, I. B. M. (eds) *Scotland: Environment and Archaeology, 8000 BC–AD 1000*, 45-62. John Wiley & Sons, Chichester.

Earwood, C (1997). Bog-butter: a Two Thousand Year History. *Journal of Irish Archaeology* **8**, 25-42.

Edwards, K J & Whittington, G (1997). Vegetation change. In Edwards, K J & Ralston, I B M (eds) *Scotland: Environment and Archaeology, 8000 BC–AD 1000*, 63-82. John Wiley & Sons, Chichester.

Edwards, K J, Whittington, G & Hirons, K R (1995). The relationship between fire and long-term wet heath development in South Uist, Outer Hebrides, Scotland. In Thompson, D B A, Hester, A J & Usher, M B (eds) *Heaths and Moorland: Cultural Landscapes*, 240-8. HMSO, Edinburgh.

Ellis, C (1998). A possible wooden platform; Carse of Stirling, Scotland, *NewsWARP* **24**, 6-8.

Ellis, C (1999a). *Archaeological Assessment of the Scottish Wetlands*. Unpublished report produced for Historic Scotland, AOC, Edinburgh.

Ellis, C (1999b). *Wetland Archaeology: Carse of Stirling Archaeological Assessment*. Unpublished report produced for Historic Scotland, AOC, Edinburgh.

Ellis, C (1999c) Wooden Structure from Carse of Stirling, *NewsWARP* **25**, 33.

Fenton, A (1970). Paring and burning and the cutting of turf and peat in Scotland. In Gailey, A & Fenton, A (eds) *The Spade in Northern and Atlantic Europe*. Ulster Folk Museum and the Institute of Irish Studies, Queen's University of Belfast, Belfast.

Finn, C (1999). Words from kept bodies. In Coles, B, Coles, J & Schou Jorgansen, M (eds) *Bog Bodies, Sacred Sites and Wetland Archaeology*, 79-84. Wetlands Archaeology Research Project, Exeter.

Frenzel, B (1983). Mires – repositories of climatic information or self-perpetuating ecosystems? In Gore, AJP (editor) *Mires: Swamp, Bog, Fen and Moor*, **A**, 35-65.

Gilbert, D, Amblard, C, Bourdier, G & Francez, A-J (1998). The microbial loop at the surface of a peatland: structure, function and impact of nutrient input. *Microbial Ecology*, **35**, 83-93.

Gimingham, C H (1972). *Ecology of Heathlands*. Chapman & Hall, London.

Grant, I F (1961). *Highland Folk Ways*. Routledge, London.

Green, M (1993). *The Gods of the Celts*. Alan Sutton, London.

Halliday, G (1997). *A Flora of Cumbria*. Centre for North-West Regional Studies, University of Lancaster.

Hingley, R (1995). The Iron Age in Atlantic Scotland: searching for the meaning of the Substantial House. In Hill, J D & Cumberpatch, C (eds) *Differing Iron Ages: Studies on the Iron Age in Temperate Europe*, 185-94. British Archaeological Reports, International 602, Oxford.

Hingley, R (1998). *Settlement and Sacrifice: the Later Prehistoric People of Scotland*. Canongate, Edinburgh.

Hingley, R, Ashmore, P, Clarke, C & Sheridan, A (1999). Peat, archaeology and palaeoecology in Scotland. In Coles, B, Coles, J & Schou Jorgansen, M (eds) *Bog Bodies, Sacred Sites and Wetland Archaeology*, 105-114. Wetlands Archaeology Research Project, Exeter.

Hulme, P D & Birnie, R V (1997). Grazing-induced degradation of blanket mire:

its measurement and management. In Tallis, J H, Meade, R & Hulme, P D (eds) *Blanket Mire Degradation: Causes, Consequences and Challenges*, 163-173 (Proceedings of Mires Research Group Conference, University of Manchester). British Ecological Society, London.

Hunter, F (1997). Iron Age hoarding in Scotland and northern England. In Gwilt, A & Haselgrove, C (eds) *Reconstructing Iron Age Societies*, 108-33. Oxbow Books, Oxford.

Ingram, H A P (1982). Size and shape in raised mire ecosystems: a geophysical model. *Nature, London*, **297**, 300-303.

Ingram, H A P (1987). Ecohydrology of Scottish peatlands. *Transactions of the Royal Society of Edinburgh: Earth Sciences*, **78**, 287-296.

Ingram, H A P (1992). Introduction to the ecohydrology of mires in the context of cultural perturbation. In Bragg, O M , Hulme, P D, Ingram, H A P & Robertson, R A (eds) *Peatland Ecosystems and Man: an Impact Assessment*, 67-93. International Peat Society, Jyväskylä.

Ingram, H A P (1997). Mires as cultural landscapes. In Parkyn, L, Stoneman, R E & Ingram, H A P (eds) *Conserving Peatlands*, 159-61. CAB International, Wallingford.

Ingram, H A P & Bragg, O M (1984). The diplotelmic mire: some hydrological consequences reviewed. *Proceedings of the 7th International Peat Congress, Dublin*, **1**, 220-234. International Peat Society, Helsinki.

Innes, J B & Shennan, I (1991). Palynology of archaeological and mire sediments from Dod, Borders Region, Scotland. *Archaeological Journal* **148,** 1-45.

Ivanov, K E (1981). *Water Movement in Mirelands*. Academic Press, London.

Mackay, K (forthcoming). History of Flanders Moss. In *Forth Naturalist and Historian* **8**.

Mallik, A U, Gimingham, C H & Rahman, A A (1984). Ecological effects of heather burning. 1 Water infiltration, moisture retention and porosity of surface soil. *Journal of Ecology* **72**, 767-76.

McCullagh, R & Tipping, R (eds) (1998). *The Lairg Project 1988-1996: The Evolution of an Archaeological Landscape in Northern Scotland*. Scottish Trust for Archaeological Research, Monograph **3**, Edinburgh.

Moore, P D (1993). The origins of blanket mire, revisited. In Chambers, F M (ed) *Climate Change and Human Impact on the Landscape*, 217-25. Chapman & Hall, London.

Oke, T R (1987). *Boundary Layer Climates* (2nd Edn). Routledge, London.

Plachter, H & Rossler, M (1995). Cultural landscapes: reconnecting culture and nature. In von Droste, B, Plachter, H & Rossler, M (eds) *Cultural Landscapes of Universal Value – Components of a Global Strategy*, 15-18. Gustav Fischer, Jena.

Pyatt, D G & John, A L (1989). Modelling volume changes in peat under conifer plantations. *Journal of Soil Science*, **40**, 695-706.

Raftery, B (1996). *Trackways Excavated in the Mountdillon Bogs, Co. Longford, 1985-1991*. (Irish Archaeological Wetland Unit, Transactions **3**). Crannog Publications, Dublin.

Rawes, M & Hobbs, R (1979). Management of semi-natural blanket bog in the northern Pennines. *Journal of Ecology*, **67**, 789-807.

RCAHMS (1990). *North-East Perth: an Archaeological Landscape*. Royal Commission on the Ancient and Historical Monuments of Scotland/HMSO, Edinburgh.

Rees, S E (1979). *Agricultural Implements of Prehistoric and Roman Britain*. British Archaeological Reports No.69, Oxford.

Romanov, V V (1968). *Hydrophysics of Bogs*. Israel Programme for Scientific Translation, Jerusalem.

Ross, A (1986). Lindow Man and the Celtic Tradition. In Stead, I M, Bourke, J B & Brothwell, D (eds) *Lindow Man: the Body in the Bog*, 162-9. British Museum, London.

Rydin, H (1987). Microdistribution of *Sphagnum* species in relation to physical environment and competition. *Symposia Biologica Hungarica*, **35**, 295-304.

Rydin, H (1993). Mechanisms of interactions among *Sphagnum* species along water-level gradients. *Advances in Bryology*, **5**, 153-185.

Sheridan, A (1996). The oldest bow ... and other objects, *Current Archaeology* **149**, 188-90.

Sjörs, H (1948). Mire vegetation in Bergslagen, Sweden. *Acta Phytogeographica Suecica*, 21, 277-290.

Smout, T C (1997). Bogs and People since 1600. In Parkyn, L, Stoneman, R E & Ingram, H A P (eds) *Conserving Peatlands*, 162-7. CAB International, Wallingford.

Staines, B W , Balharry, R & Welch, D (1995). Moorland management and impacts of red deer. In Thompson, D B A, Hester, A J & Usher, M B *Heaths and Moorland: Cultural Landscapes*, 294-308. HMSO, Edinburgh.

Stead, I M, Bourke, J B & Brothwell, D (eds) (1986), *Lindow Man: the Body in the Bog*. British Museum, London.

Stewart, A J & Lance, A N (1983). Moor draining: a review of impacts on land use. *Journal of Environmental Management*, **17**, 81-99.

Tansley, AG (1939). *The British Islands and their Vegetation*. Cambridge University Press, Cambridge.

Taylor, JA (1983). The peatlands of Great Britain and Ireland. In Gore, AJP (editor) *Mires: Swamp, Bog, Fen and Moor*, **B**, 1-46.

Taylor, J A & Smith, R T (1972). Climatic peat – a misnomer? *Proceedings of the Fourth International Peat Congress, Helsinki* **1**, 471-84.

Thomas, B & Trinder, N (1947). The ash components of some moorland plants. *Empire Journal of Experimental Agriculture*, **15**, 237-248.

Thompson, D B A & Miles, J (1995). Heath and Moorland: some conclusions and questions about environmental change. In Thompson, D B A, Hester, A J & Usher, M B (eds) *Heaths and Moorland: Cultural Landscapes*, 362-85. HMSO, Edinburgh.

Tipping, R 1994. The form and fate of Scotland's woodlands. *PSAS* **124**, 1-54.

Turner, R C & Briggs, C S (1986). The bog burials of Britain and Ireland. In Stead, I M, Bourke, J B & Brothwell, D (eds), *Lindow Man: the Body in the Bog*, 144-61. British Museum, London.

Turner, R C & Scaife R G (1995). *Bog Bodies: New Discoveries and New Perspectives*. British Museum, London.

Whittington, G & Edwards, K J (1997). Climate Change. In Edwards, K J & Ralston, I B M (eds) *Scotland: Environment and Archaeology, 8000 BC–AD 1000*, 11-22. John Wiley, Chichester.

7

Trying to Understand Woods

ALAN HAMPSON AND CHRIS SMOUT

'Nature is man's ancestral home and nurse . . . landscape his modern mirror'
– MAX NICHOLSON, THE ENVIRONMENTAL REVOLUTION

INTRODUCTION

The belief at the root of this essay is that historians and scientists need each other in trying to understand past and present environments, and that this is nowhere better exemplified than in studies of woods and trees in the historical landscape. The present condition of woodland is the result of past processes, both natural and ecological, human and historical, so that it is not possible to understand woods without ecologists considering the part that the hand of man has played, or historians considering the constraints nature placed upon human activity. The future condition of woods, equally importantly, cannot be planned in the landscape regardless of ecological and social factors, or regardless of what the past has done to mould those factors.

The question of whether or not human activity has a legitimate place in a concept of the natural world is perhaps one of the most fundamental questions for conservationists. Though it too often goes by default, it has been at the heart of many of the great conservation debates, such as those originating in the days of John Muir over the extent to which the big national parks in America should be managed. In Scotland, at least, it is not possible to understand woods without considering the part that the people have played in their development and history. Woods are dynamic, they regenerate, mature and gradually senesce, albeit on a long timescale. This natural cycle is not only influenced by a range of environmental factors. The woodland cover that has developed since the end of the last glaciation has done so throughout in the presence of man.

We have no clear idea how Mesolithic people used or modified woodland as hunter gatherers, during the four millennia of their existence in Scotland, from about nine thousand years ago, but it would be surprising if they had no impact. Percentages of hazel pollen, for example, rise dramatically at different times during this period, and it has been suggested that the growth of hazel was deliberately encouraged as a scrub useful for food and for light construction purposes. Neolithic man, as the first farmers, began on a large scale to turn the wildwood into wood pasture, and to clear spaces for crops. The Bronze Age and the Iron Age carried clearance to such extremes that it is now generally accepted that the Lowlands at least were already open country over large areas when the Romans came (Tipping, 1994). We know less about woodland cover in the Dark Ages, though it has been suggested that in Fife the presence and withdrawal of the Romans coincided with a temporary re-invasion of tree cover (Whittington and Edwards, 1994). Little more is known about the Middle Ages, but available evidence makes it clear that woodland was managed both as hunting reserve and as economic resource. By 1500, Scotland was short of large, accessible building timber. From the evidence that exists, there can be little doubt that by 1750 woodland cover had already been restricted to one of the lowest in Europe, possibly at around four per cent of the land surface, but quite intensive use and management thereafter did not reduce it below three per cent (Smout, 1993; Smout and Watson, 1997). Hence, all the woods that remain are likely to have been heavily manipulated and modified by human activity. Since the middle of the last century the percentage of tree cover has gradually increased to 17 per cent thanks to the establishment of conifer plantations, some of it on the site of earlier woods.

What is natural about present-day tree cover? The extent and pattern of tree cover is not natural. The wider landscape within which it sits has been highly manipulated and influenced by human activity. This often results in a diverse mosaic of habitats with increased area of edge and the associated richness and abundance of biodiversity. On the other hand, the small size of many of the semi-natural woods that remain may result in island biogeographical effects, with a diminished number of species, or with species at high risk of local extinction. The situation is exacerbated in other ways. Sporting estates achieve excessive deer numbers by feeding them as if they were domestic stock or pets, and sheep-farming is subsidised for every mouth on the hill. The result is a highly unnatural situation of artificially high grazing levels and concomitant poverty of regeneration.

UNDERSTANDING THE PRESENT CONDITION OF WOODS

In trying to understand woods, it is important to consider not just the ecological processes going on in the wood at present but also past and current human influences. Indeed, it is often this broader context that scientists find so difficult to explain. For example, why does a wood have a peculiar species composition or why are certain expected features not present? Increasingly, it is being realised that there might not be an ecological reason, but what is commonly referred to as 'the result of past management'.

The west-coast oakwoods provide a good illustration. To the ecological eye today they often appear unexpectedly uniform, but a historian can explain that this is a recent development. Dugald Clerk of Braleckan, in Argyll, described the trees on his farm as ash, elm, birch, hazel, alder, rowan, gean, aspen, willow, hawthorn and blackthorn, which belonged to him, and the oak, which belonged to his feudal superior, the Duke of Argyll (NLS, 1751). He went on:

> All these different species of woods of which your Grace's oaks in most places make but the smallest share, are so intermixed and grow so thick and close together in the form of a hedge or one continual thicket, galling, rubbing upon and smothering one another for want of due weeding and pruning that it is morally impossible for any person to enter into these thickets to cut or weed either your Grace's oaks, or my other woods without at the same time breaking or cutting less or more of the other in order to get access to these thickets.

This document provides a species list of the wood (as well as an impression of its structure) which is completely at variance with what is seen in Argyll today. Many woodland felling contracts of the eighteenth century contain similar lists of species diversity.

What happened can be seen from the advice provided early in the nineteenth century by forestry experts like Robert Monteath, anxious to maximise the produce of the woods for charcoal burning and, especially, tan barking. As he wrote in 1827:

> Oak, and nothing but oak, is the only profitable tree for coppice cuttings, and whenever such a plan is intended, nothing else should be reared.

The result was a monoculture of oak, often planted from acorns on open ground, or on openings in pre-existing oakwoods. The provenance of the acorns was often English, which was considered superior to the native Scottish, giving rise to a mixture of sessile and pedunculate oak, or hybrids between the two. For one reason or another, oak seems to have problems in regenerating to maturity over most of its British range today, but part of the difficulty in these west-coast oakwoods may relate to genetic problems involving seed of unsuitable provenance for the environment.

Conversely, ecologists can explain why certain species grow where they do and the range of species that could potentially grow on particular sites. They might also be able to explain why certain species of plants or animals are not present, perhaps because their habitat requirements are not met. For instance, it has been recently argued (Crawford, 1997) that the explanation for the absence or poor performance of trees over much of north-western Scotland may be in the onset of oceanicity of the climate since the Bronze Age, possibly in fatal combination with the hand of man. As Hingley and Ingram have shown in the previous chapter, ground may become waterlogged both through climate change and through human removal of tree cover. If it does, tree seeds have a hard time.

Recent studies at Coniston in Cumbria (Barker, 1998) also show how the historian's and ecologist's arts can be complementary. On the wooded hillsides, the most valuable areas for nature conservation are the gorges, where such species as small-leafed lime, wood fescue and tucsan survive out of reach of grazing and with a nutrient supply undamaged by human activity. On the interfluvial slopes, a combination of grazing by domestic animals and a history of long-term coppicing that has removed nutrients, results in a greatly impoverished flora beneath the still-existing canopy of oaks. Nevertheless, the Coniston basin still has 35 per cent semi-natural woodland coverage, compared to 5 per cent for Cumbria as a whole.

History often demonstrates that the reason why many woods survived to the present is because they have been valued, not because they have escaped attention. Sometimes it was the shelter they provided, especially in winter, which was prized, along with the flush of grass and herbs in summer. Sometimes it was the timber for charcoal, tanbark, tool-making and construction – this could involve coppicing or pollarding. Sometimes it was their use for sport that was paramount, as a medieval hunting forest or a Victorian pheasant convert. Sometimes they were valued for their associations, a Wallace oak; or their beauty, like the glade of pine round Loch-an-Eilein which was preserved from felling for aesthetic reasons (Smout, 1994).

Each form of value would mean a different use and probably a further deviation from the natural original; whether it was the rotational openings associated with coppicing or the snowberry understorey associated with pheasant coverts. And value does not always mean wise use. Overwintering cattle can bring an ancient wood gradually to grief, of which there are documented examples back to the eighteenth century (Smout and Watson, 1997). Coppicing can have costs to the nutrient base and the ability of the site to continue high yields of timber indefinitely, probably worse in areas of high rainfall but noticed in Scotland in the past as far east as Perthshire. So valuing and using a wood for human purposes can have quite fundamental impacts on its character. But surely value is almost a pre-requisite for wise use: no value, and the woods are eradicated as worthless encumbrances on the ground, only surviving if they are virtually inaccessible to people and their stock. Instances of preservation due to remoteness certainly occur in Scotland, but they tend to be small in scale, like the aspens on the screes of Glen Esk or the Scots pines at Callart on Loch Leven. The first steps to ensuring the future of our woods is to understand why there are valued.

DECIDING HOW TO MANAGE WOODS

The above suggests that even taking a non-intervention approach will not result in a natural wood because too much human intervention has occurred in the past and is bound to occur in the future. At Coniston, in the coppiced areas, non-intervention is unlikely to bring back the small-leafed lime and other scarce plants because the nutrient level is not right, and even if sheep could be fenced out, the wood is likely to be modified by human-introduced species like rabbits which could not be excluded. This is not to say that a non-intervention approach is invalid, just that the wood would still be subject to a range of human influences.

Very often, in practice, some form of intervention is required if the wood is to be retained. In minimising intervention to achieve the desired objectives (even if these objectives are concerned with maintaining the ecological interest and processes within the wood) there is already an element of choice introduced. For example, if grazing pressure is preventing regeneration, the exact modified level of grazing decided upon will determine the character of the wood which develops, both in terms of its structure and its species composition.

A good example can be found currently in Glen Finglas in the Trossachs, where the Woodland Trust has come into the ownership of the relics of a medieval royal hunting forest. 'No trees, no deer' was the declaration of those responsible for managing it in the early eighteenth century – itself a fascinating sidelight on the contemporary view of the association of deer with woods, since a hundred and fifty years later, red deer in Scotland were firmly associated with heather moorland rather than woods (Fiona Watson, *pers. comm.*). There was, however, even then, competition between game preservation and farming, with a great many local tenant farmers anxious to graze their animals in the wood pasture associated with the deer. After about 1750, the farmers obtained free run of the glen, apparently giving many of the trees a rough pollarding in order to obtain wood just out of reach of animals browsing the regrowth, a practice known elsewhere in Scotland as 'cutting high'. In due course, rural depopulation gave the wood entirely over to sheep, but it survived, albeit somewhat reduced in size and density, to the present day, and with little maturing regeneration but abundant seed-fall on the ground.

This wood is, therefore, still a woodland pasture and has been so for centuries. It has considerable nature conservation interest – it is in the top rank of woods in Scotland for its lichen flora, if one leaves aside the exceptional woods of the Atlantic-seaboard. It has great interest as a cultural landscape. It is possibly Scotland's only survival of woodland landscape associated with a royal forest, and also with a vanished peasant woodland-management practice.

The Woodland Trust wishes in its management of this area to do three things: firstly, to maintain and enhance the wood for its lichens and other floral interest, which means maintaining an appropriate space between the trees as well as the trees themselves. Secondly, to maintain for as long as possible the general appearance and character of the wood as a cultural landscape with its distinctive pollarding. Thirdly, to encourage natural regeneration to the degree which will ensure that there is still a wood there in the future, but within limits which will allow the other two objectives. In practice, this means maintaining it as wood pasture with a carefully controlled level of grazing by sheep and cattle, and possibly in future reintroducing some form of pollarding at least to demonstrate the nature of the old technique.

Excluding animals from a wood might seem always to be the first step in good management, but this example shows that other choices might be better, depending on the objectives of management in the first place. Rassall National Nature Reserve in Wester Ross demonstrates very clearly how a simple management choice can transform a wood in three or four decades. The name of this famous northerly ash-wood itself implies that it was grazed by stallions, so its history of use is of great antiquity. When it was acquired by the Nature Conservancy it was subject to heavy sheep grazing, was very open and with little regeneration – clearly a wood pasture under pressure. It was then fenced in two ways. An outer perimeter fence excluded domestic animals but not deer. The inner fence was intended to exclude all grazing animals. Within that innermost enclosure, the wood now is almost impenetrable, the old ashes swallowed up by younger trees and by hazel scrub; between the two enclosures, the open character is preserved, with a certain amount of regeneration and great swathes of bracken. If the purpose of the management plan is to show what would happen under different grazing régimes, it succeeds brilliantly. If the plan has other objectives, it is unclear what they might be. A new management plan might legitimately seek to reinstate the 'ash-wood of the stallions' over all or part of the area as a medieval cultural landscape grazed with horses. But it could also have other objectives. Rather than trying to lay down rules about what particular types of wood should be like, there is a need to make considered decisions about the desired future condition of individual woods, having regard to their history, to the wishes of the present day and to the possible options. Only having done this, is it possible to set in train the management prescriptions necessary to achieve the desired state.

With woods which are primarily valued for their biodiversity this might especially involve ensuring that the conditions in the wood are maintained so as to perpetuate or enhance the features of species interest currently extant. In some woods part of the interest may well be in the fact that there has been little disturbance to these woods in recent times. With others this may be their prime value, but respect should still be paid to remnants of cultural history such as charcoal-burning platforms. Moreover, in a great many there is likely to be some flexibility over the species composition and structure which gives scope to incorporate a broader range of objectives.

Woods might equally well be seen to be primarily of value for their cultural interests, which must include a great deal of policy planting, not least of the Victorian period. The splendid Wellingtonias, silver firs, Sitka spruce, Douglas fir, incense cedars and monkey-puzzles that often surround nineteenth-century houses in the Highland and Lowlands alike deserve sympathetic management and judicious replacement where the originals have come to grief, partly because of their outstanding contribution to the landscape, partly because of their frequent historical associations with the original plant collectors such as David Douglas himself. The time is also overdue for ecologists to take them more seriously as habitat. The most casual bird-watcher knows them to be a sure refuge for high numbers of coal-tits, tree creepers and goldcrests but there must be more to it than that. The flora that develops as decades pass and the woods are restructured will be quite different from what they are now.

HOW TO DETERMINE THE DESIRED RANGE OF OBJECTIVES

Traditionally, foresters tended to manage woods for timber while conservationists managed them for their ecological interest. Recent moves to a multi-benefit approach reflect a growing desire on the part of society as a whole to see woods delivering a greater range of benefits in a more integrated way. There is also growing recognition of some of the broader roles that tree cover could play, such as helping in flood control through regulating hydrological processes.

While policy and practice have undoubtedly moved in a more flexible direction, there have only been limited moves to open up the process of deciding on the range of benefits that any particular wood could deliver. At present, public bodies tend to have a very strong influence, either through the status attributed to particular woods or through the nature of the incentives offered for management. It is often argued that this is democratic, in that these bodies are implementing policy of the elected Government. Increasingly, however, people wish to be involved in determining what happens to woods in their locality. This is just starting to open up a whole new and fascinating area. The Local Biodiversity Action Plan Process is an early example of a mechanism set up to enable local preferences to be taken into account.

Part of the reason why there tends to be scientific concern over the idea of involving the general public in making such decisions, is a notion that the public might have only a limited understanding of the situation, perhaps based on myth and folklore. The romantic idea of the Great Wood of Caledon is a good example of this. Until the middle of the nineteenth century there was little emphasis on the ghost of a great wood covering Scotland, except for the occasional reference back to the Elizabethan topographer Camden, who relied on the slightly earlier Boece, who in turn had fantasised from an over-imaginative reading of classical authors. The myth takes its modern form first in the writings of the Sobieski Stuarts, those myth-mongers of the high Victorian period. They injected into it the essential elements of Germanic forest myth – it had been huge, wild and recent. From them the story passed, through nineteenth and early twentieth-century hands (such as Skene, Nairne and Ritchie), but not much changed in its essence, to Frank Fraser Darling and Reforesting Scotland, gathering popular and political momentum on its way. With the help of palynology and a closer reading of historical and archaeological sources, this view began to be revised (Smout, 1994, 2000). The discovery that there had indeed been such a wood, but that it had begun to decline five millennia ago for natural as well as human reasons, presents a more realistic picture. One way to help the general public to share this picture and to contribute to it in important ways would be to involve them in projects to write their own community woodland histories.

An approach which takes public opinion into account suggests a changing role for the scientist, from one of essentially setting the agenda and using a range of mechanisms to deliver it, to one of helping to inform and facilitate a more open and inclusive process, for example, by suggesting the likely outcomes of particular scenarios. It may also assist in achieving a better integration of objectives. By and large, most scientists are trained to think along sectorial lines, whereas the lay person tends to pick what they like or are interested in. For example, many conservationists are puritanical when it comes to the place of exotic species. The public tend to be more accepting of the contribution they can make to the landscape and of their value as habitat. Such things need to be taken into consideration when trying fully to understand and evaluate woods.

Finally, one of the clear lessons we should learn from history is that the value attached to woods is likely to continue changing, reflecting the changing nature of society. Thus, in developing a vision of the future role that woods might play, there is considerable merit in a broad approach which will leave future generations with the flexibility to derive the range of benefits they most desire.

References

Baker, S. (1998). The history of the Coniston woodlands, Cumbria, UK. In *The Ecological History of European Forests*, Kirby, K.J. and Watkins, C. (eds.), Wallingford, 167-84.

Crawford, R.M.M. (1997). Oceanicity and the ecological disadvantages of warm winters. *Botanical Journal of Scotland*, 49 (2), 205-22.

Monteath, R. (1827). *Miscellaneous Reports on Woods and Plantations*, Dundee.

NLS (1751). National Library of Scotland MS 176-85, f. 66.

Smout, C. (1993). Woodland history before 1750. In *Scotland since Prehistory: Natural Change and Human Impact*, Smout, T.C. (ed.), Aberdeen.

Smout, T.C. (1994). Trees as historic landscapes: Wallace's Oak to Reforesting Scotland. *Scottish Forestry*, 48, 244-52.

Smout, T.C. (2000). *Nature Contested: Environmental History in Scotland and Northern England since 1600*, Edinburgh.

Tipping, R. (1994). The form and fate of Scotland's woodlands. *Proc. Soc. Antiq. Scot.*, 124, 55-65.

Whittington, G. and Edwards K.J. (1994). Palynology as a predictive tool in archaeology. *Proc. Soc. Antiq. Scot.*, 124, 65-?

Other books of interest from Scottish Cultural Press . . .

The Cairngorm Gateway
ANN GLEN
ISBN: 1 84017 027 1

Fragile Environments
The use and management of Tentsmuir National Nature Reserve, Fife
GRAEME WHITTINGTON (ED.)
ISBN: 1 898218 77 3

The History of Soils and Field Systems
S FOSTER AND T C SMOUT (EDS)
ISBN: 1 898218 13 7

The Nature of Fife
Wildlife and Ecology
GORDON B CORBET (ED.)
ISBN: 1 84017 008 5

Rothiemurchus
T C SMOUT AND R A LAMBERT
ISBN: 1 84017 033 6

Scotland since Prehistory
Natural Change and Human Impact
T C SMOUT (ED.)
ISBN: 1 898218 03 X

Scotland's Rural Land Use Agencies
DONALD G MACKAY
ISBN: 1 898218 31 5

Scottish Woodland History
T C SMOUT (ED.)
ISBN: 1 898218 53 6

Species History in Scotand
T C SMOUT (ED.)
ISBN: 1 84017 011 5

find out about these books and others on our website:
www.scottishbooks.com

PLATE 1: *Vertical aerial photograph of Newcastleton, Liddesdale, Dumfries & Galloway*
(CROWN COPYRIGHT: RCAHMS)

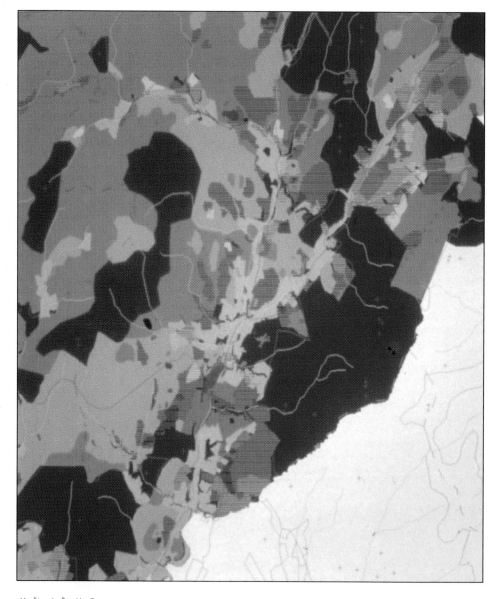

PLATE 2:
*Current land-use
in upper Liddesdale,
Dumfries & Galloway*
(CROWN COPYRIGHT:
RCAHMS)

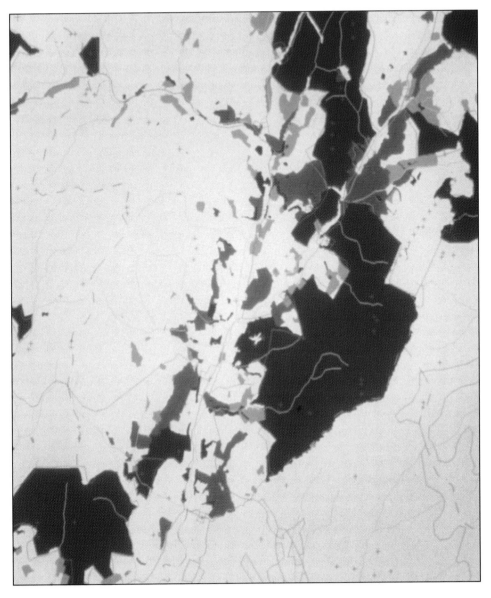

PLATE 3: *Relict historic land-use and forestry plantations in upper Liddesdale, Dumfries & Galloway* (CROWN COPYRIGHT: RCAHMS)

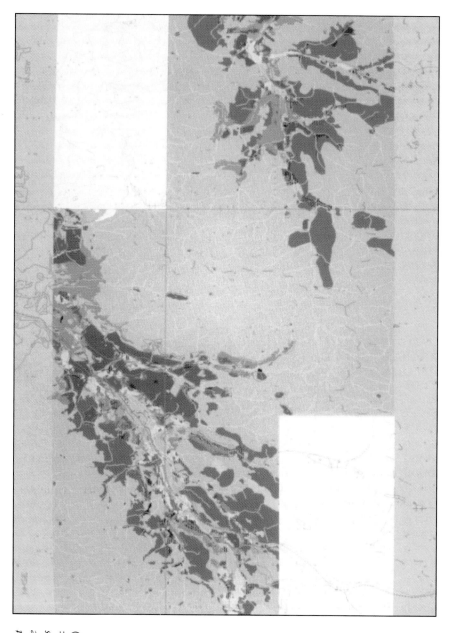

PLATE 4: *Current land-use in the western Cairngorms* (CROWN COPYRIGHT: RCAHMS)

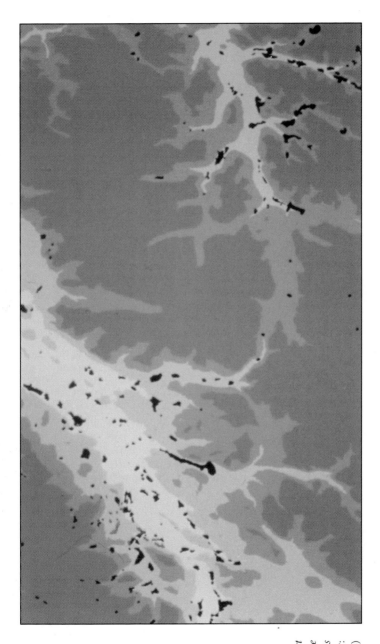

PLATE 5: *Relict land-use in the western Cairngorms* (CROWN COPYRIGHT: RCAHMS)

PLATE 6: *Vertical aerial photograph of north-east Fife. Tentsmuir, top right* (CROWN COPYRIGHT: RCAHMS)

PLATE 7: *Current land-use in north-east Fife* (CROWN COPYRIGHT: RCAHMS)

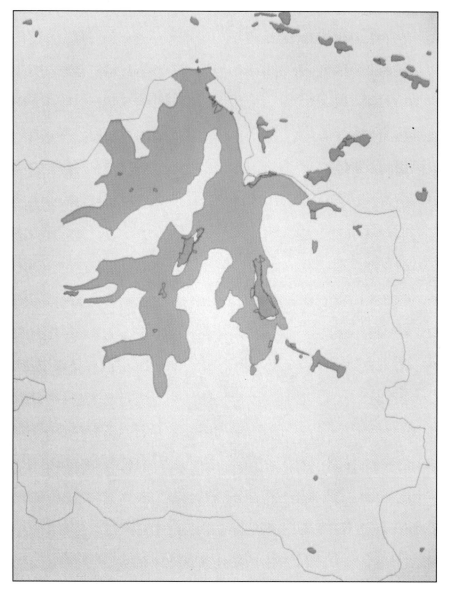

PLATE 8: *Mar Lodge Estate, current woodland (green) and post-medieval settlement (pink)* (CROWN COPYRIGHT: RCAHMS)

PLATE 9: *Cropmark landscape, Leuchars, north-east Fife* (CROWN COPYRIGHT: RCAHMS)

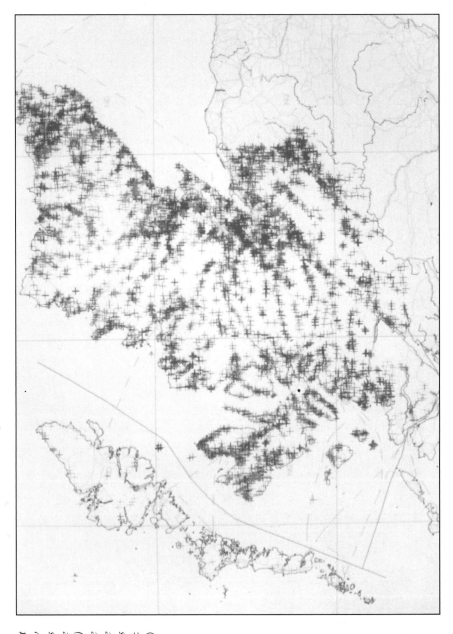

PLATE 10: *First Edition Survey Project: buildings recorded in the NMRS before (red) and after (blue) the survey of the northern counties* (CROWN COPYRIGHT: RCAHMS)

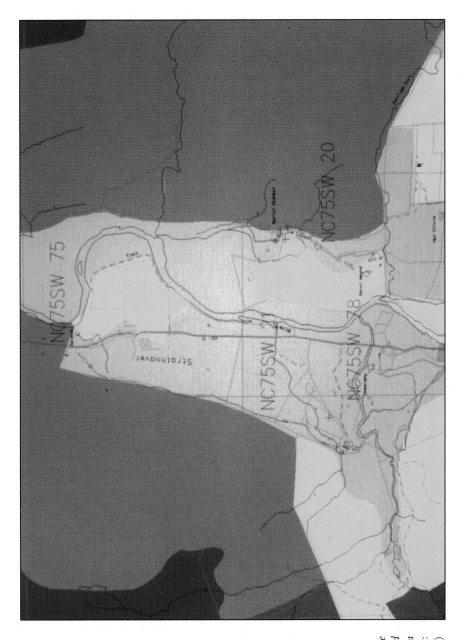

PLATE 11: *Land-use in Strathnaver, based on Macaulay data*
(CROWN COPYRIGHT: RCAHMS)

PLATE 12:
Oblique aerial view of the remains of Haywood, Lanarkshire (CROWN COPYRIGHT: RCAHMS)

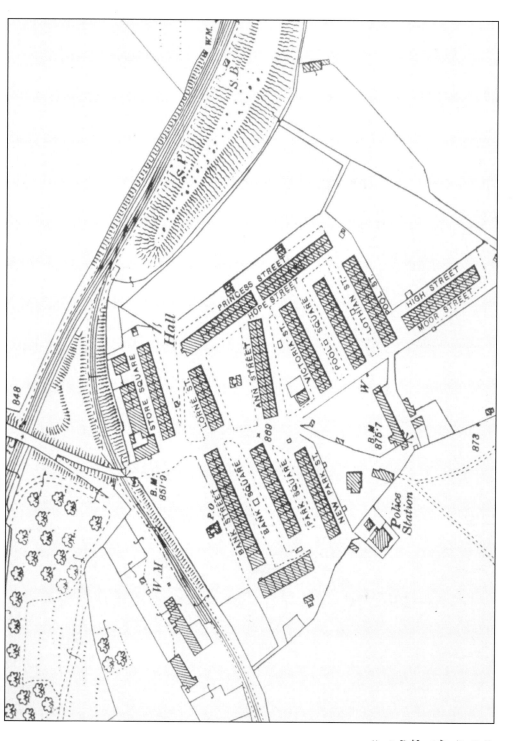

PLATE 13: *Haywood, composite plan based on OS 1:2500 map, 1897* (CROWN COPYRIGHT: RCAHMS)

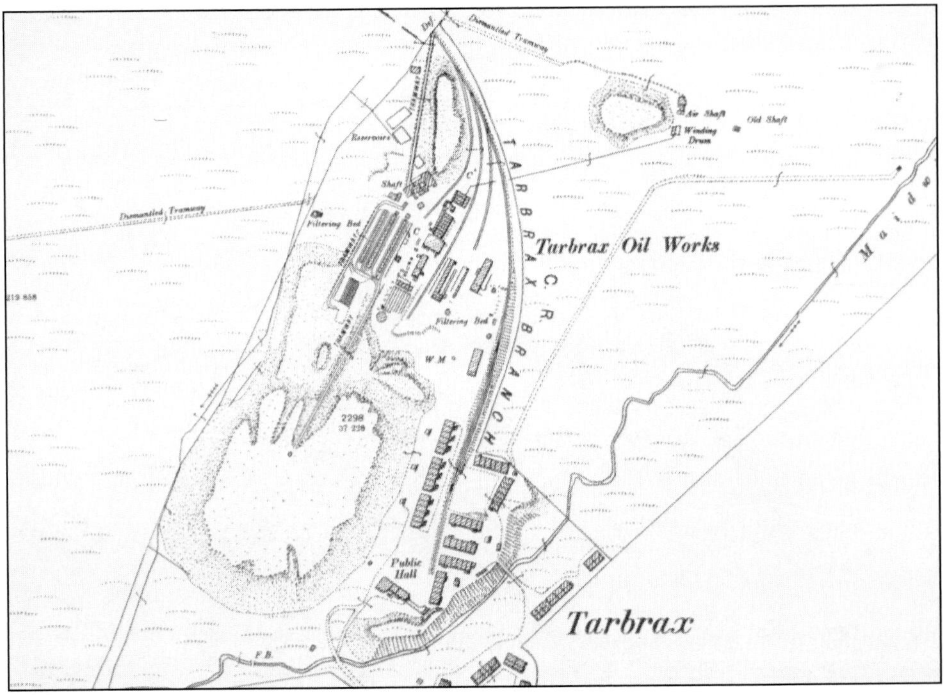

PLATE 14: *Tarbrax Oil-shale Works, based on OS 1:2500 map, 1897*
(CROWN COPYRIGHT: RCAHMS)

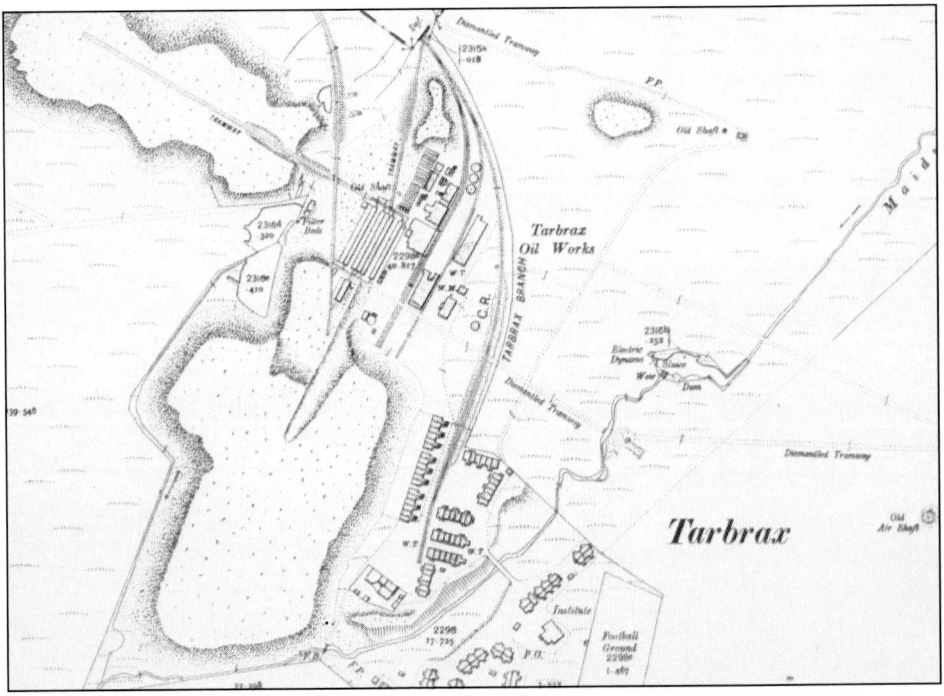

PLATE 15: *Tarbrax Oil-shale Works, based on OS 1:2500 map, 1·911*
(CROWN COPYRIGHT: RCAHMS)

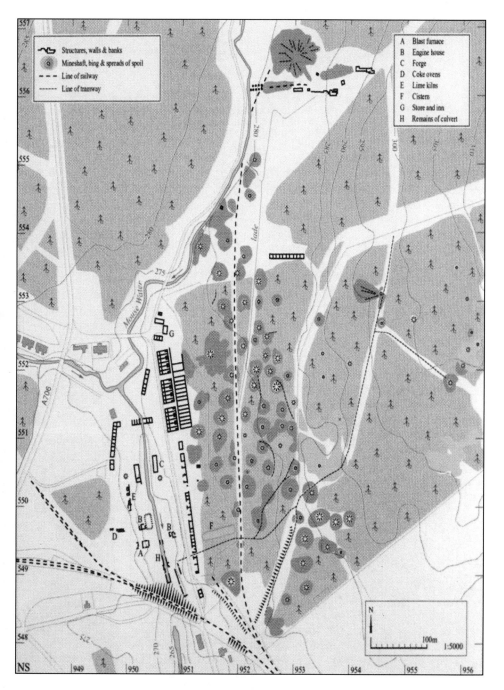

PLATE 17: *Map showing farmsteads and rig-and-furrow cultivation
in part of the Central Scotland Woodland*
(CROWN COPYRIGHT: RCAHMS)